THE ESSENCE OF

BUDDHISM

ROY GILLETT

Published in 2001 by Caxton Editions
20 Bloomsbury Street
London WC1B 3JH
a member of the Caxton Publishing Group

Designed and produced for Caxton Editions
by Open Door Limited
Rutland, United Kingdom

Editing: Mary Morton
Coordination and Typesetting: Jane Booth

Title: Buddhism
ISBN: 1 84067 300 1

Acknowledgments:
TIBET IMAGES: p.4, 5, 6, 7, 8, 10, 14, 21, 24, 25, 31, 38, 52, 62, 63, 66, 71, 74, 81, 82, 88, 92, (Ian Cumming); p. 12 (Wendy Dison); p. 15 (Norman Joseph); p. 9, 16, 50(Diane Barker); p. 11, 54 (Stone Routes); p. 37, (Jamie Hunter); p. 91 (Kim Yesli); p. 69 (Mani Lama); p. 73 (Yeo Dong Wan); p. 77 (Raphaele De Mandre)

THE ESSENCE OF BUDDHISM

ROY GILLETT

CAXTON EDITIONS

CONTENTS

INTRODUCTION – THE ORIGINS OF TIBETAN BUDDHISM

Far right: a view of Sanye monastery with prayer flags.

Below: a Buddhist wall painting.

"The Tibetans combine the best qualities of both the western and eastern characters", remarked a seasoned traveller to McLeod Ganj, the headquarters of HH The Dalai Lama of Tibet in exile. He was trying to describe how they combine the detached, non-interfering attitude of most westerners, with the deep, inclusive spirituality more often associated with easterners.

Certainly Tibetans can seem to us to be a mass of contradictions. They are a deeply religious people, but so unpretentious that monks fidget and drink tea during the most sacred ceremonies. These ceremonies are the longest and most intricate imaginable. High lamas argue for the privilege of who will be last rather than first. Prostration and constant repetition of mantra dominates the practice. Yet, the deeper one reaches in to the meaning of the practices, the less there is left to find, or worship. Tibetan Buddhism has many methods and intricate debating arguments. All are designed to de-intellectualise the mind – exactly the opposite to the effect of western education. There are as many methods to clear delusion, as there are delusions. 84,000 have been identified. The relief is that we do not have to address the delusions we do not have. While prepared to tame the most complex minds, Tibetan Buddhism is of and for simple souls.

What follows is a brief introduction to Buddhism and a deeper outline of the Tibetan way of teaching it. It is only possible to select from this profoundly rich field in so short a book, but the aim is to do more than merely scratch the surface. The main chapters follow the Lam Rim, or Graduated Path to Enlightenment. The Lam Rim is designed to explain the main issues of life in a way that makes us really check up and experience them. If we follow the path, then we will not only grasp the idea, but also begin to realise its implications – that we can change our lives for the better.

Shakyamuni Buddha lived between 500 to 600 years before Christ. He was born Siddhartha, the son of a king. The circumstances of his birth were exceptional. It is said that his mother, Queen Maya, visualised her conception as the painless entering into her of a six-tusked, god-like white elephant. She gave birth in the standing position, supporting herself on a Sal tree. Siddhartha was given every comfort. His father instructed that Siddhartha only be allowed to see young and beautiful things. At the age of 29 years, he avoided the guards, travelled outside the palace and saw an old suffering man for the first time.

Right: a painting of Shakyamuni Buddha, Norbulingka Institute, near Dharamasala Himachal Pradesh, India.

As a result, Siddhartha gave up everything to wander, meditate and search for an explanation of all experiences in our sense-based lives – *samsara*. He tried a range of methods, including extreme ascetic denial. Finally, at the age of 35, he determined not to move from beneath the bodhi tree at Bodh Gaya, until he became enlightened. This climaxed in a night of extreme horror and temptation. Refusing to be intimidated either by the most seductive or the most foul of experiences, he realised the middle way and achieved enlightenment.

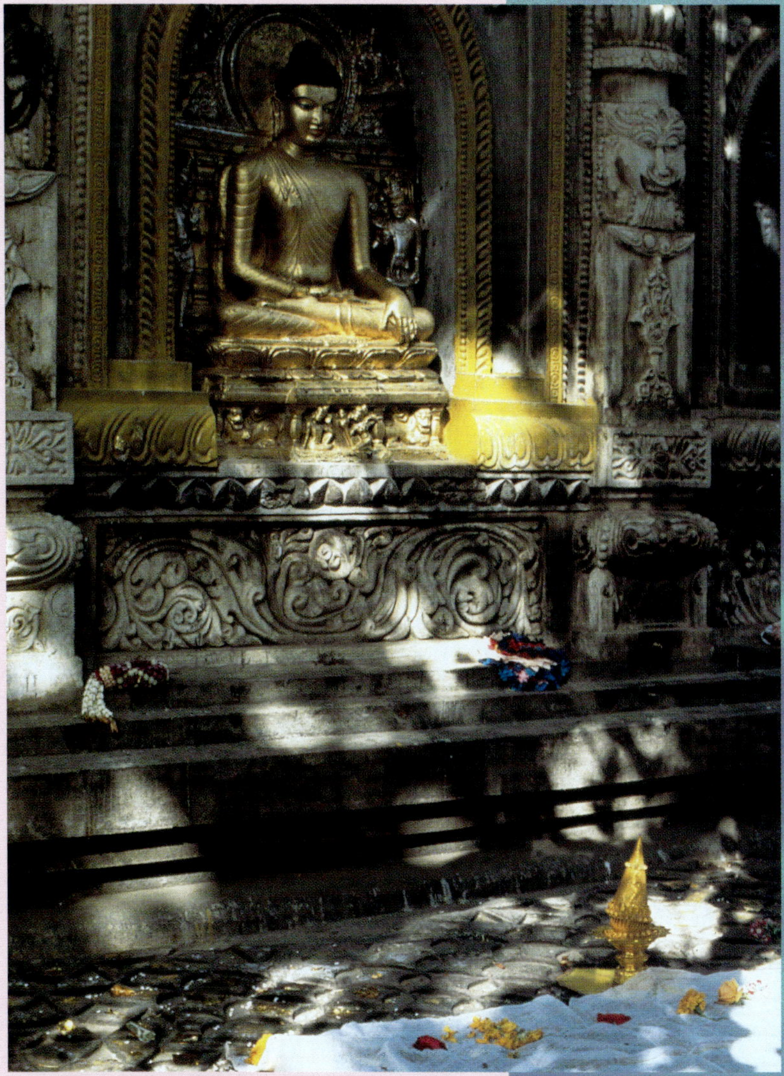

Above: under the bodhi tree at Bodh Gaya, India.

Enlightenment means to have a mind that sees clearly the essential suffering nature of every day samsaric existence and the way of liberation from that suffering. Buddha taught this understanding to his first disciples at Sarnath near Varanasi – a few hundred miles north of Bodh Gaya. He continued to travel throughout Bihar to gather and ordain followers – the Sangha – and to teach until he was 80 years old. Weakened by dysentery, the Buddha gave teachings and ordinations to the very last. Finally, in a Sal grove at Kushinagara, he lay on his right side, left his physical body and passed into Mahaparinivana – the great state beyond even the bliss of nirvana.

The Buddha specifically left no successor. In his last days, he said to Ananda, his chief disciple, "Therefore, O Ananda, be ye lamps unto yourselves. Be ye a refuge to yourselves. Betake yourself to no external refuge. Hold fast to the truth as a lamp."

Although they show great respect for teachers and the lineage of teachers that have passed down the teachings, Buddhists do not bow to any person. Nor do they bow to the many statues and representations in the Buddhist tradition themselves. Rather disciples bow to the essential truth that these individuals and images represent. To cross a river, it may be necessary to use a boat, but once on the other side we do not continue to carry the boat on our backs. Paradoxically, for all its images and saints, Buddhism is unique in that its ultimate reality is not a God. Buddhism's ultimate truth is Sunyata – emptiness that is empty of its own emptiness – no beginning, no end. Shakyamuni Buddha's disciples taught the way out of suffering to this enlightened truth of existence. Like a breath of fresh air, Buddhism spread rapidly through India, then into what is now Sri Lanka, Thailand, Korea, Indo China, China, Mongolia and Japan.

Below: monks at an early morning ceremony at Nechung Monastery, Tibet.

As did Jesus Christ, the Buddha accepted all classes and conditions of people. He looked with compassion on all creatures, animals, insects, even the beings that lived in plants and rocks and in all realms beyond the world as we know it. Such teachings of charity, compassion and inclusiveness gained ground in place of the ritual and sacrifice of the Hindu Vedic traditions of the time. This flourishing can be seen at the Ajanta and Ellora cave carvings and on many other stupas (archetypal buildings representing a perfect universe), temples and statues constructed in the centuries after the Buddha's passing. It incorporated a rich tantric (ritual) tradition. This was especially focused at Nalanda University in Bihar State. Here more than 10,000 students and 1,000 teachers learnt and practised a wide curriculum of Buddhist scriptures, ceremonies, tantric and magical techniques until the 12th century AD. It is said that when Bakhtiyar Khalji destroyed the monastery it took six months to burn.

Above: seventh century releif wall carvings at Palhalupuk temple, Lhasa, central Tibet.

Below: ancient writing carved in stone; Marsyandi valley, Manang, Nepal.

A thousand years earlier the origins of our western knowledge were themselves being burnt at the library in Alexandria. The Roman Empire was falling and Europe plunging into and then struggling out of the Dark Ages. At this time, the construction of Buddhist stupas, statues and carvings marked the flourishing of Shakyamuni's teaching in Asia. Fortunately, in spite of Bakhtiyar Khalji's actions, this knowledge was preserved in its entirety. In the early 7th century AD, the Emperor Songtsen Gambo transformed the feudal militarism of Tibet. He sent scholars to India to learn Sanskrit, create a written Tibetan language and bring Mahayana Buddhist artefacts to his country. His successors continued the work, so that by the end of the 8th century the first monastery was established at Samye. All branches of mathematics, poetry and medicine, government, art and architecture were cultivated, alongside the philosophy and psychology of Buddhism.

The spiritual heroism of Padmasambhava (Guru-Rinpoche) tamed the demons of the shamanistic Bon Po practices. Atisha's gentle incisive Lam Rim established powerful foundation teachings. Overall, knowledge that had grown for 1,300 years came from Nalanda and much further afield to Tibet. Here it was enshrined, preserved and grew into a long and rich monastic tradition that itself has lasted more than 1,200 years until today. In all, Tibetan Buddhism represents a rich treasure of wisdom, with an unbroken lineage of 2,500 years. The cannon of this lineage and mass of knowledge is written in the books of the Kanjur.

Tibetan Buddhism is unique in that it is the only one of the Buddhist traditions that includes all of the three vehicles towards enlightenment– the Hinayana, Mahayana and Vajrayana (or Tantra).

The Hinayana (or lesser) vehicle focuses on the Buddha's basic teachings of the Four Noble Truths, Death and Rebirth, Karma, the way of liberation through taking refuge in Buddha, Dharma and Sangha, meditation and the practice of the virtuous life to achieve enlightenment.

Below: Tibetan cymbals for use when meditating.

Above: ceremony at Nechung Monastery, Tibet.

The Mahayana (or greater) vehicle adds to the above a very strong motivation of Bodhicitta – caring for others before one's self. The Bodhisattva takes a vow for eternity (all lifetimes) that he or she will not achieve enlightenment until all other beings in samsara are enlightened. This strong motivation to put others before self is seen as the essential quality of the truly enlightened mind.

The Vajrayana (or Tantra) vehicle involves a magical process of transforming sensual phenomena into the service of Bodhicitta to accelerate the process of helping all sentient beings towards enlight-enment.

At its height through the centuries leading to the Chinese occupation 1950 to1959, a majority of the male population spent a substantial part of their lives in monasteries; the wheel was only used for prayer. Evidence of prayer and dedication in stones, flags, temples and stupas dominated all parts of the country. Buddhist principles of non-harming directed most social practices. Hunting, fishing and mining were discouraged strongly and hardly happened. The head of state, His Holiness The Dalai Lama, was seen as the incarnation of Chenrezig – the Buddha of compassion.

The years since the Chinese invasion have seen a rededication of Buddha Dharma. Its culture, which seemed about to be lost in the 1960s, has experienced a major renaissance, not only in India where most Tibetan exiles settled, but among idealists in all walks of life throughout the world. Hundreds of study and meditation centres have been founded all over the world. In percentage terms, Tibetan Buddhism is one of the world's fastest-growing religions.

Below: Mani prayer stones, Tibet.

The attraction is threefold: the simple compassionate humility of its leader HH The Dalai Lama; the breadth and rich variety (purely disciplined magic) of its practice; and its depth of clear and logical philosophical analysis. With these three, it seems to be offering just what is missing in modern society: a leader beyond self-interest that you can trust; a surge of experience that takes you beyond day-to-day limitations; and a system of analysis that puts in perspective the half truths that struggle against each other for power in our modern societies.

Below: His Holiness the Dalai Lama at Kalachakra, Jispa, Zanskar, India in 1994.

There is little (if anything) in our modern world that is not made easier to bear and possible to solve by applying some aspect of the Tibetan Buddhist (Dharma) teachings. The pages that follow outline these teachings and are full of examples of how we can practise and use them in our everyday lives.

To gain maximum understanding, it is important to suspend disbelief and give the ideas a chance to rest and relate to each other in your mind for a while. There is no need to have faith, or belief. If, having given a little time to check them out, you find the images, reflections and ideas helpful, then you will wish to use them in your life. If, however, you find them unacceptable and/or of no use, just put them to one side.

"Mind is beginningless because it is mind".

Pramanavartika

Below: whatever the situation, things generally turn out better when everyone's mind is attuned and we all work together.

"Are we all of the same mind then?" is the frequently asked question at the end of a long discussion. Whether we have been comparing notes, planning a campaign of action in business, or on the football field, things turn out better when everyone's mind is attuned and we all work together.

The Buddhist view goes further. Really, there is only one mind. This mind is beginningless and, if we clear away the confusion caused by hanging on to egocentric delusions, everyone will realise this. Because mind is beginningless, it cannot be possessed, given or taken in whole or part between people. Nor is it shared really. True mind is clear, knowing and common to all. There never was a time when it did not exist – nor will there ever be a time, when it will not exist.

This view of mind may seem to put Buddhist philosophy at odds with modern materialistic science, which seeks to devise laboratory experiments to prove that mind is entirely dependent on the physical brain. This view also holds that a particular genetic structure is the root cause of everything, by creating that brain and other bodily characteristics. This seems convincing, but let us try a little Tibetan debating analysis of the thesis to see if it has any really logical foundation.

At first sight, this "courageous" and "realistic" modern view seems very convincing, but it is essentially flawed for three reasons. Firstly, if mind started with genetic structure and the physical brain determined by it, what created the genetic structure? Secondly, if minds are separate, different and imperfect in their performance, how can the experiments devised by the imperfect minds of the scientists determine a perfect truth about them? Thirdly and conversely, if there is a "scientific" mind that sees the physical brain and its genetic structure perfectly, why has it not created perfect minds for everyone and, if it did, would not this prove that there was just one perfect beginningless mind in the first place? So, genetics, while invaluable in describing the way relative life is built and fits together, cannot describe or define mind, because it is dependent upon it.

Below: Buddhist philosophy is at odds with modern materialistic science, which seeks to devise laboratory experiments to prove that mind is entirely dependent on the physical brain.

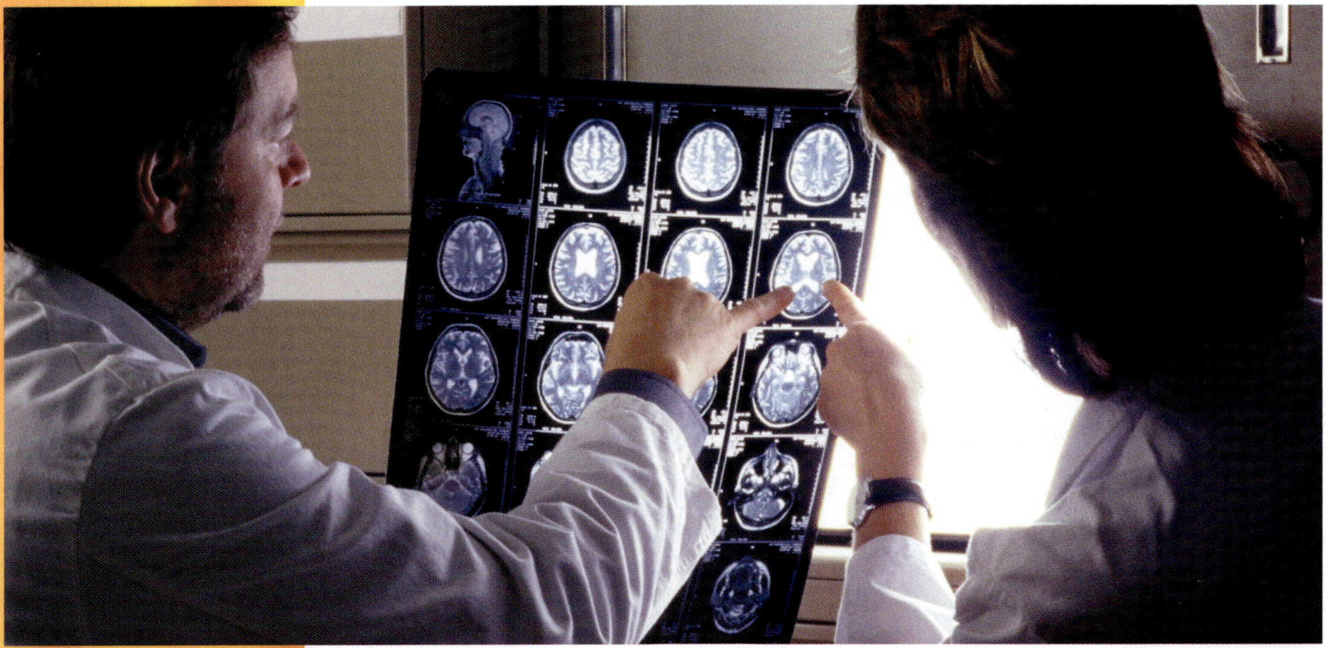

To realise that we are all of the same mind, that is beginningless and clear, is a great cause for every one of us to celebrate without ceasing. For no one is damned. There will always be hope for everyone. To be clear, happy and understand things as they really are, it is just a question of our clearing the muddied "windows" of delusion, which make us see ourselves as separate from and threatened by others.

We should grasp this opportunity without delay. By being born human and with our faculties to read or hear the Buddhist teachings (having a "Perfect Human Rebirth" as the Dharma teachings call it), we are born with the greatest good fortune imaginable – to see things clearly and so liberate ourselves from suffering. Such an opportunity is rare. As Shantideva put it in his *The Way of the Bodhisattva*:

> *"Just as a flash of lightning on a dark, cloudy night*
> *For an instant brightly illuminates all,*
> *Likewise in this world, through the might of Buddha,*
> *A wholesome thought rarely and briefly appears."*

Above: to be clear, happy and understand things as they really are, it is just a question of our clearing the muddied "windows" of delusion.

Far right: a Heavenly musician or 'Yul-khor-bsrung' playing the lute; a wall painting at Depung Monastery, Tibet.

So many things could have prevented us knowing about the information in this book. We could have lived in a country or been born in a time, where only one religion was allowed. Maybe we were illiterate, or blind and deaf. Maybe our life was so full of hunger, poverty, sickness, hard work, or distracting and corrupt friends that we could not find the time to consider the teachings.

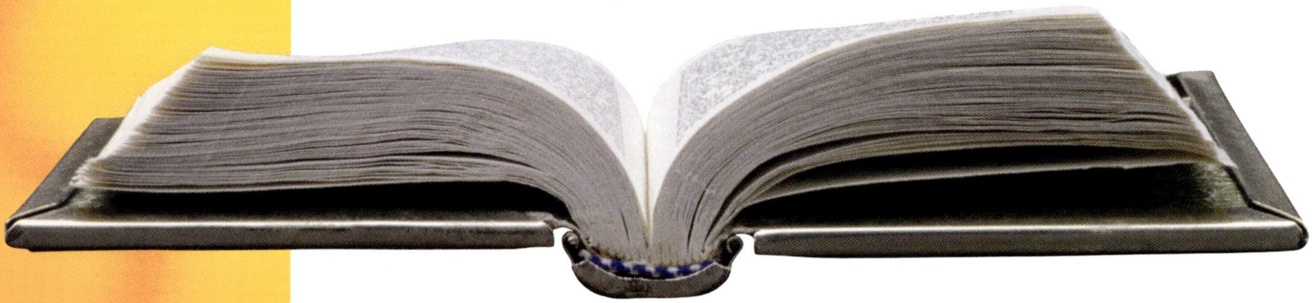

If we extend the possibilities to the Buddhist concept of reincarnation, we could have been born an animal. While animals are part of the same beginningless mind and show characteristics of kindness, loyalty and sensitive social behaviour, most are trapped in difficult bodies and the struggle for territory and material survival. In the wild, there is always the danger of being eaten – the distraction of being constantly on one's guard. We may have been born in the realm of the "Hungry Ghosts". Here experience is dominated by the impossibility of satisfying needs, or in the constant torment of the Hell Realms.

Just as bad, we could have been born in a condition of directionless wealth, where one indulgence after another was constantly satisfied without effort. Then, we would have been so exhausted by our indulgences, we could not see beyond them. Perhaps we could have been born with perfect bodies, or special talents that led to our being constantly scrutinised and admired. Then we would never have been given time to make decisions in our lives.

Instead of all the above unfortunate possibilities, we have been born able to read, or at least hear a reading from, a book like this.

Right: a reflection you may wish to try...
It would be helpful to sit in a quiet place and spend a little time thinking about people less fortunate than yourself or caught up in sensuality, alcohol, drug and sexual abuse and obsessions.

A reflection you may wish to try...
It would be helpful to sit in a quiet place and spend a little time thinking about people less fortunate than yourself. Think of people in poor parts of the world, in hospitals, the disabled, those working long hours. Think of people caught up in sensuality, alcohol, drug and sexual abuse and obsessions – and where this might lead them. Then think of people, who are richer than you – are they happier? Do you think their happiness will last?

Visualise a turtle swimming along the floor of an ocean, which can just see the light of the surface above. Floating on that surface is a golden ring. It is as likely for you to find the information in this book, as it is for the turtle to find its neck in that golden ring, when it floats to the surface.

"All worldly activities are like husks".

Lama Tsong Khapa

Who wants to be unhappy? We spend most of our lives trying to avoid it, but can we ever succeed?

When buying clothes we want to be sure not only that they fit and are comfortable, but also that people will admire us in them. Yet, even if the choice is perfect, in a few weeks or months fashions will change and the outfit that filled us with so much pride has to be discarded and replaced. It is our wedding anniversary – a chance to celebrate at a luxury restaurant. We make the booking and dress for the occasion. Now come the many pitfalls that might "spoil the evening". Are we placed at the wrong table, next to noisy people, or rushing waiters? The menu reads seductively and we are hungry, but will the starter match the main course, and how much should we spend? Even if money is no object, will buying the most expensive item seem the right decision after we have eaten it? Then comes the wait for food. Is someone else being served before us? Will we be able to attract the waiter for the sweet course? Will the coffee be cold, before the liqueur is served? Are we paying too much for the wine? Are we too full? We pay the bill (will the free mints ever be enough to assuage our sense of shock!?) and go home. Given the ingredients, the money we have spent, the crowding and the waiting, could we not have created a much better meal and enjoyed even more luxury, if we had stayed at home? Even if we had, would over-indulgence have led to our being sick, or collapsing drunk, "missing the fun" we were anticipating. Then there is the problem of the morning after!

Above: a celebration in a luxury restaurant has many pitfalls which can spoil the enjoyment.

Far right: the Potala at dawn, Lhasa, Tibet.

Below: three young monks in ceremonial dress, Langmusi Monastery, Gansu province, China.

Talking like this is what puts people off Buddhism! "Why do they have to be so pessimistic? Buddhists don't know how to enjoy themselves." The Buddha would reply "By all means do, or have what you wish, but does this doing or having really make you happy?" Indeed, the Buddha would go further. "It is not so much what we do, or what we have that causes unhappiness, but our **attachment** to it". This is the essential paradox of life. Sensual experience ceases to be pleasurable, when we crave for its coming, being and going. If we can take it or leave it, we will not suffer, because we will see things as they are. The mind becomes clear; we act appropriately. We are not a problem to others and are not seen as a problem by them.

"The proof of the pudding is in the eating!" People, who have lived with Tibetan Buddhist lamas and monks, even visitors to ordinary lay families, are often struck by how easy the day-to-day interactions of living together are. There is a refreshing lack of resentment, emotional manipulation and hidden agendas. One does not feel judged, or indulged – rather left to make one's own decisions. Things are as they are. People glory in the success and happiness of others. They try to help, but rarely interfere. All this comes from an uncluttered understanding of reality. Life is suffering. We are all in it together. Let us take care to avoid creating suffering and make every effort to ease it, whether it occurs in humans, animals, plants or the very fabric of the earth and all that is made from it. Such caring mindfulness really lightens the burdens of everyday life. For all their material problems, there is much smiling and heartfelt laughter in Tibetan communities.

Left: if striving for success is going to lead to unhappiness, why try to succeed at work, or in sport? Indeed, why support a football or any other team?

Such a way of thinking and living is really revolutionary, because it challenges many assumptions and systems upon which modern materialistic society is based. If striving for success is going to lead to unhappiness, why try to succeed at work, or in sport? Indeed, why support a football or any other team? In their hearts, England football supporters have understood this for many years. Our civil legal system is based on the assumption of responsibility and redress for wrongs. If attachment to experience is the root cause of unhappiness, how can the agony of legal struggle lead to happiness and, if it does for a moment, how long will that moment last?

We think that lasting happiness is not only possible, but is our right. "Someone else must be responsible" if such happiness is denied us. This delusion is the root cause of our dependence on scientific and other "experts" in the modern world. There is an underlying assumption that we do not have to take responsibility for many areas of our lives – e.g. how we care for our bodies, what we eat, where we go, how we get there. If things go wrong, someone else must be identified and punished. Such an attitude keeps our minds like those of spoilt, demanding children – the prey of skillful marketing and populist political campaigns – prone to "road rage" in the struggle for survival and a sensual "lasting happiness", we can never have.

Left: the mind that is trapped in sensual need is never satisfied. Greed constantly arises.

The mind that is trapped in this sensual need is never satisfied. Greed constantly arises. In ignorance we blame others for our failures – our parents, our teachers, the people across the road, "my boss does not like me, (my sex, race, or religion etc. etc.) ". The blaming grows into hatred, a view of "them" and "us". The news, entertainment and advertising media encourage, oversimplify and exploit our greed, ignorance and hatred. We find ourselves trapped in a sea of suffering dissatisfaction. Buddhists say the world, where people are attached to finding happiness through material things, has always been like this. They call it *samsara*.

The Buddhist approach liberates us from samsara. The root cause of our suffering is that we are attached to sensual pleasure that does not and cannot last. By its very nature sensual pleasure is impermanent. Ice cream melts and, even if it did not, if we ate too much, we would soon be sick! After sexual orgasm, there is the rest of our lives. When we accept this, we enjoy the coming and going of sensual pleasure for what it is, not what it might and should be. Indeed, we may well try harder and become more productive, because we do everything we do for its own sake, without resentment and struggle. We see more clearly. We are more effective. We allow the muddy confusion of expectation and desire to settle down within us and become clear.

A reflection you may wish to try… It would be helpful to sit in a quiet place and imagine yourself floating up out of your body and looking down on yourself and the world around you, as it goes about its normal business. It is as if you were watching a film of your own and other people's lives – maybe re-run recent events from this perspective. Notice how everyone is becoming caught up in emotional afflictions, yet are unaware of what is happening to them.

"If you knew how hard it is to acquire,
Living the average life would be impossible.
If you saw its great benefits,
You would be sorry if it stayed meaningless.
If you thought about death,
You would make preparations for your future lives.
If you thought about cause and effect,
You would stop being reckless."

Lama Tsong Khapa

Far left: the Buddhist approach liberates us from samsara enabling us to enjoy the coming and going of sensual pleasure for what it is, not what it might and should be.

The world most of us live in seems designed to protect us from facing up to the inevitability of death. Many people would say that just writing the previous sentence is being unnecessarily morbid. Death is something to be compartmentalised, tucked away and covered up. Funeral arrangements are discreet. We are not expected to see dead bodies, as we walk along the street in our day-to-day lives – just in tragic news reports, or film dramas from "far away". If deaths do occur, there are people quickly on hand to take away and "hide" the evidence.

Below: the world most of us live in seems designed to protect us from facing up to the inevitability of death.

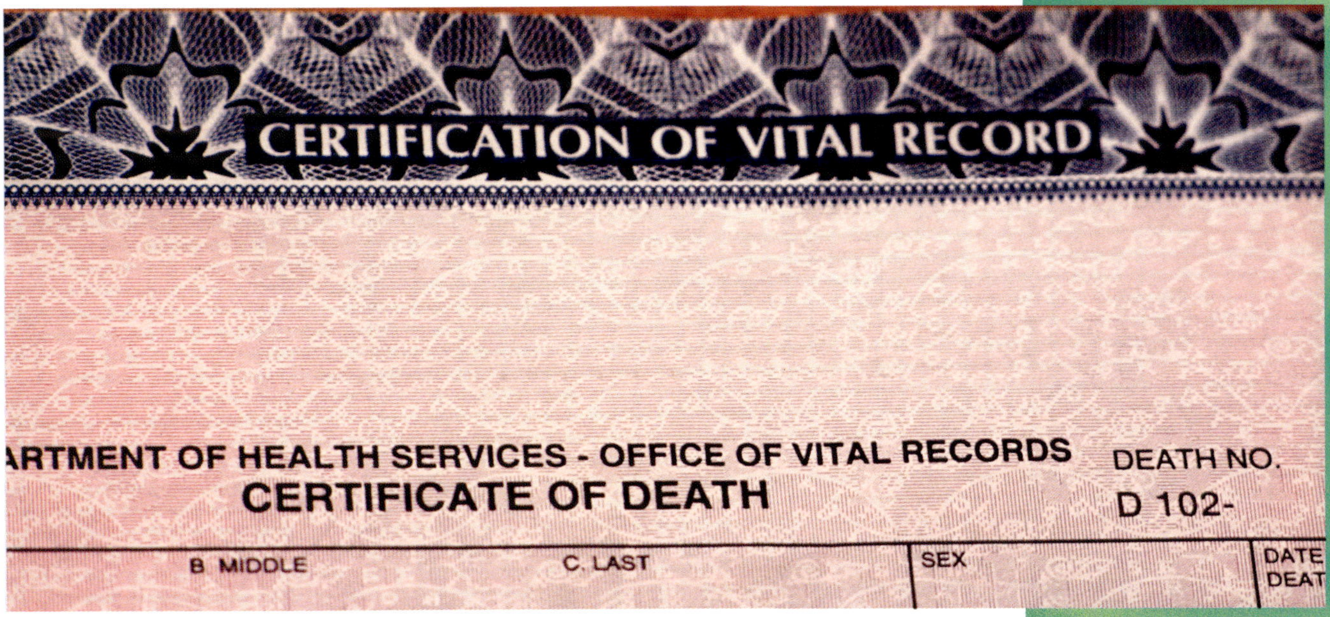

CERTIFICATION OF VITAL RECORD
ARTMENT OF HEALTH SERVICES - OFFICE OF VITAL RECORDS
DEATH NO.
CERTIFICATE OF DEATH
D 102-
B. MIDDLE
C. LAST
SEX
DATE

Above: horror movie-makers and theme-park ride designers play on the fear of death unmercifully, but without realism.

Realising the inevitability of death is a nightmare experience for most people. Horror movie-makers and theme-park ride designers play on these fears unmercifully, but without realism. For when the film and ride end all the real people remain alive and are unlikely to be wiser about the real death experience. Indeed, they are very likely to be less wise! It is a fact that one hundred years from now all but a handful of the people living today will be dead. There is no power in the Universe that can stop this. However rich, strong, powerful, wise and even magical we are, death will come. Every moment we live, every breath we take brings it closer. Nor can we be certain of when it will come. Very young people can die. Even healthy people can die before sick people. We can be cut off in the middle of major plans. Accidents, catastrophes, even things that usually help us to live such as food, or medicine can kill us. Our bodies are frail – they will not last.

Tibetan lamas have documented the actual stages of the death process in great detail. They can tell you exactly the order and way that each of the senses fade, as the various elements dissolve, and then, if attention is held, the mind can focus on clear light. From this clear light vision consciousness can pass back through the stages of dissolution in reverse order. As soon as this reverse process begins various stages of rebirth commence, firstly in the "Bardo", the Tibetan word for this intermediate state, then in a new physical incarnation.

Tibetan Buddhist death meditations are designed to prepare for this experience. We are told that consciousness can rest in clear light. There are stories of high lamas sitting after death in a state of "suspended animation" with no bodily decay for several weeks. There is a tradition of consciously reincarnated "Tulkus", where a previously deceased lama is recognised in the body of a child. H H The Dalai Lama is the best-known example today – see Chapter 10. There are scores of others and some amazing anecdotes. A couple of months before the much loved Lama Thubten Yeshe died, in 1984, he gave instructions that repairs to the damaged bodywork of the meditation centre's Land Rover be undertaken. When Lama Osel, his recognised reincarnation, first visited the centre as a toddler, he repeatedly pointed to the damage that was still not repaired.

Below: an old man at prayers, Leh Monastery, Ladakh, India.

Below: Karma is considered to carry on through many lifetimes in a constant process of reincarnation, until the mind is cleansed and of absolute, enlightened clarity.

Driving the process is the state of mind of the dying person. To remain consciously aware we have to be fully prepared for the death experience and without attachments. Someone tormented with fear, anger, hatred, resentment, guilt, or any kind of desperate need cannot have the open-minded acceptance to recognise what is happening. The struggle for survival will lead to swooning into uncontrolled darkness, only to re-awaken without any memory in a new incarnation.

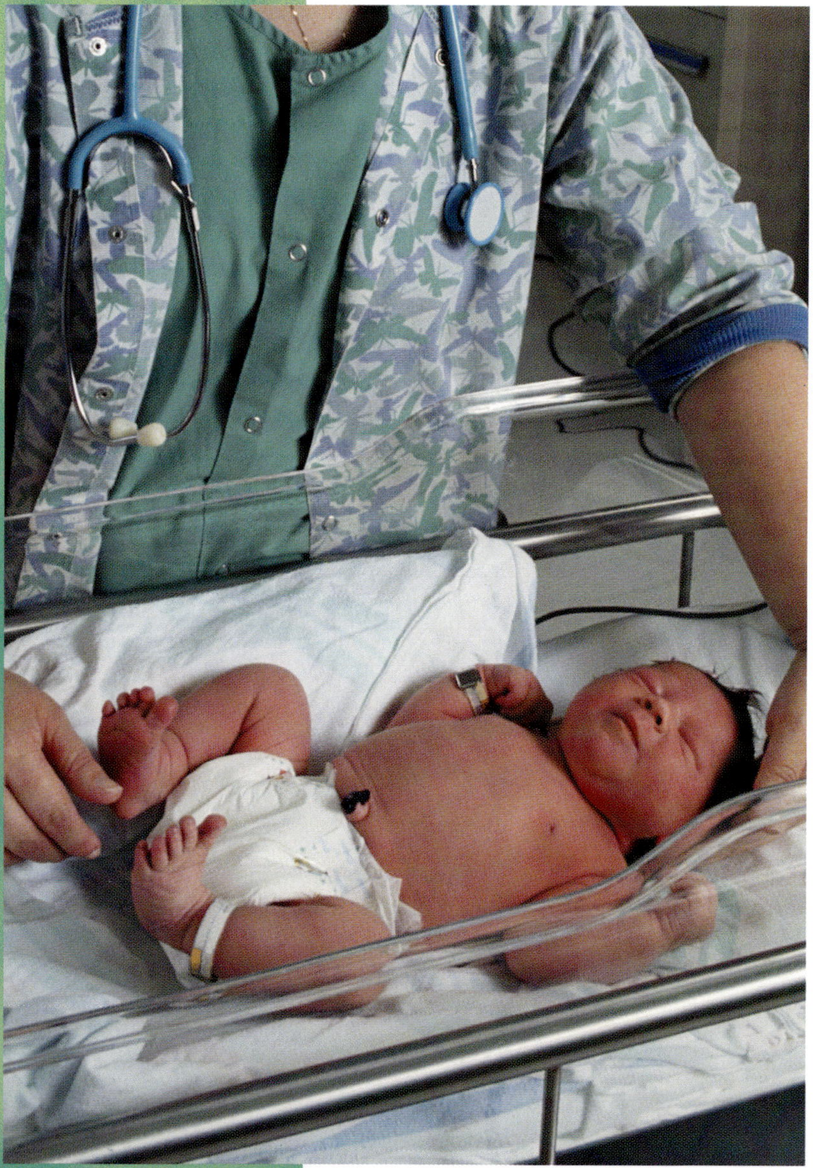

The whole process is controlled by the supreme and just logic of Karma – the law of cause and effect that takes account of every thought, word and deed throughout and between all lifetimes. Contrary to some misunderstandings in western society, Karma is not about fatalism, or "copping out" of one's responsibilities. Quite the opposite – the Law of Karma says that everything we think, say and do forms an imprint on the mind. Negative thoughts, words and deeds cloud and confuse the mind and move us away from the clear light of the pure Buddha mind. As a result, we are drawn towards negative situations, experiences and attitudes. When death comes, the sum total of negativity in our mind automatically attracts us through the swoon of darkness to a new life that suits that negativity exactly.

This can include the physical and personal circumstances of the new life. If we have abused our own or other people's possessions in the present lifetime, we may be born in a world of famine in the future one. If in addition we have shown extreme kindness in a lifetime before that, we may be born in a world of famine, but be the leader who finds food for his people. It is this mixture of negative and positive karma that explains why beautifully natured people can be born with great difficulties or disablement.

The Law of Karma and the Christian view of sin seem similar, but there are two vital distinctions. Firstly, Karma is considered to carry on through many lifetimes in a constant process of reincarnation, until the mind is cleansed and of absolute, enlightened clarity. Secondly, karma is about cause and effect, not guilt. Certainly recognising and getting our minds straight about the consequences of bad actions is important.

Buddhist teachings go into graphic detail about the many levels of intensely suffering rebirths. Many meditations encourage precise visualisation of every kind of hot, cold and swamp-infested hell. Hungry ghost beings have stomachs like mountains, but food channels are blocked with glass and limbs are as thin as grass. Animal or human rebirths can lead to one being constantly eaten, or exploited and abused by others. Yet guilt is never used to motivate. Rather, the facts are clear, the choice is yours. Why be so ignorant as to choose such suffering for yourself and others?

Above: if we have abused our own or other people's possessions in the present lifetime, we may be born in a world of famine in the future one.

Below: doing things that help others and make them happy helps to clear the mind. However, doing a good deed does not create a kind of karmic credit to balance off a future, or past negative act.

Nor to the Buddhist does being born in great difficulties in this lifetime mean nothing can be done until the next lifetime. Quite the opposite – the worse the circumstances, the better we can progress – provided we can hear and understand and we act to put things right in every way possible. The Tibetans outline a very clear, logical step-by-step way of doing this.

Negative acts are created in stages of intensity – having the intention to act, performing the action and celebrating the action. The earlier in the process we stop, the less the negativity. To purify a past negative act it is necessary to recognise we acted in this way, to regret the action, to apologise and seek to put it right. Perhaps we steal an object. Firstly, we admit to ourselves we did this and it was wrong. Then we own up to the person we stole from and replace the object. To go some way along this process of purification can help. On the positive side, doing things that help others and make them happy helps to clear the mind. However, doing a good deed does not create a kind of karmic credit to balance off a future, or past negative act. All negative acts have to be worked through and purified. Rather it is that doing any positive act so clears the mind that we can recognise our negative acts and purify them. Whenever we act correctly, however badly the world seems to be treating us, we cleanse our minds and so come closer to enlightenment.

Above: whether we find it easy to accept the notion of rebirth over many lifetimes, or not, the teachings about death, Karma and rebirth are incredibly valuable in the lifetime we are living now.

Whether we find it easy to accept the notion of rebirth over many lifetimes, or not, the teachings about death, Karma and rebirth are incredibly valuable in the lifetime we are living now. Whoever we are and wherever we go, we are constantly faced with deathlike changes. We leave the home and go to school, then a new school, a university, or a new job. Perhaps a parent or close friend dies; the relationship with our lover or partner breaks up. We lose that vital league game and become relegated; our opponents succeed in an election. We lose our address book, or purse. So many major and minor events are like death.

Right: recognising and putting right our own failings and being compassionate toward others when they let us down is basic to our being respected.

We are strong, clear and successful in this one life, if we can take all these things in our stride and start again all the wiser for the experience. Recognising and putting right our own failings and being compassionate toward others when they let us down is basic to our being respected. When we accept that no negative act can ever pass unpunished in the end, it is easier to feel compassion. The thief lives constantly in fear of being stolen from, the hunter of being hunted, the murderer of being murdered, the brute of being brutalised, the liar lied to. Who would choose to live in a world of constant thievery, brutality and deception? Whether the future life of suffering is an actual rebirth or not, negative acts delude and bring suffering to the creator's mind right away. Positive acts bring great happiness.

"Do not think a small bad act
Will not return in your future lives.
Just as falling drops of water
Will fill a large container,
The little bad acts
A churl accumulates
Will completely overwhelm him.

Do not think a small virtue
Will not return in your future lives.
Just as falling drops of water
Will fill a large container,
The little virtues
The steadfast accumulate
Will completely overwhelm them."

The Buddha

"Who will protect me from these great terrors? With staring eyes I'll scour the four directions looking for a refuge. But when I see no refuge in the four directions I will give way to utter despair. If these places have no refuge, what will I do then?"

Shantideva

Below: Statue of Buddha; Kathmandu, Nepal.

The "up front", uncompromising way that Tibetan Buddhists encourage us to meditate and visualise the real experience of death and its unavoidable nature can be really frightening. Inexperienced meditators have found themselves consumed with panic. In the middle of the night, one disciple phoned his lama desperate for help. "You have to understand that you will die, but you are not dead yet," was the lama's response.

Left: by letting go of this constant anxiety about death and every other thing in life that we fear "might happen", we leave our minds clear to deal appropriately with what is happening right now.

Far left: the Wheel of Life at Ganden Monastery, Tibet.

There are lots of reasons why this is a brilliant reply. Firstly, it is certain that the disciple is "not dead yet". This is crucial. If he is not dead what has he got to worry about? If he has no reason to worry now, how does he know he will have reason to worry in the future? Perhaps, when death comes he will be so ready for it that he will cope with it, in the same way as he hopes to cope with his next breath and the one after that. By letting go of this constant anxiety about death and every other thing in life that we fear "might happen", we leave our minds clear to deal appropriately with what is happening right now.

At the same time, the answer does not allow the disciple to "cop out". He is told, "you will die". Nor does it reassure him falsely by saying it will be all right when he dies – that is unmentioned and so left open. It may or may not be all right, when he dies. All will depend on his state of mind. Clearly there is no room for complacency. Without panic, but with a focused sense of urgency, it is vital we find a refuge that will protect us and guide us through the experience of death. If we do not, we will have no control over what happens then, or at any other time in our lives. We will be lost and distracted and no real use to anyone.

From earlier chapters, it is clear that however far we look to the north, south, east and west of our world, we will only find temporary sense-based experience, which is impermanent and useless at death. We seek a level of consciousness that is clear and can make us clear, because it sees beyond sensuality. We seek wisdom that is impartial, available to all and helps everyone equally, without fear or favour. We seek a being who knows the consequences of all karmic actions and causes of all karmic results, the wishes, predispositions, scope, spiritual paths, way of liberation, previous lives, rebirth process and abandoned obstacles of all beings. We seek a consciousness that is pleasing, gentle, never forgetting, profoundly realistic, never deceived, aware of spiritual readiness, always well intentioned, keen, mindful, single-pointed, without prejudice, always aware and enlightened.

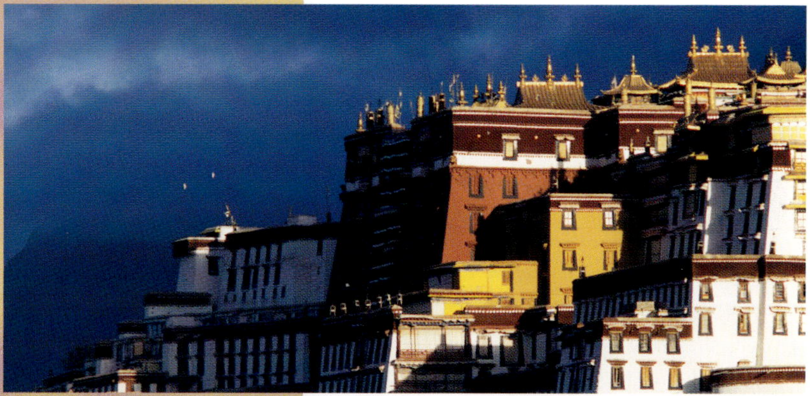

We seek one who sees the past, present and future without being attached to, or hindered by it. Only the Buddha has all of these qualities. By taking refuge in Buddha, the way his understanding leads us and other people who follow this way – Buddha, Dharma and Sangha – we move into such good company, that we are clear, beyond fear and our lives know happiness that can never fade.

It is important to insist on every single detail in the previous paragraph. Without every detail, it cannot be Buddha and so is not a suitable refuge. In our hard-sell society, we are constantly being persuaded to take refuge in sweet sounding "solutions" and objects that quickly disappoint and sour. So many of our problems arise from this. Many people's lives consist almost entirely of constantly disappointing refuge-taking. Buddhism is different. It does not seek blind faith, or anything for itself, to manipulate you with sensual satisfaction, or to pile up more and more converts. Rather Buddhism is an understanding for you to use, if it helps.

Buddha, Dharma and Sangha are the three legs of the Buddhist stool. Dharma is the way things really are. It is like a boat we need to get in and a way of behaving we have to adopt in our daily life. Buddha, who demonstrated enlightenment in the events of his life and in his teachings, is the captain. Sangha are the others in the boat. By being on the right way, with the right guide in the company of the right people, our refuge is sure.

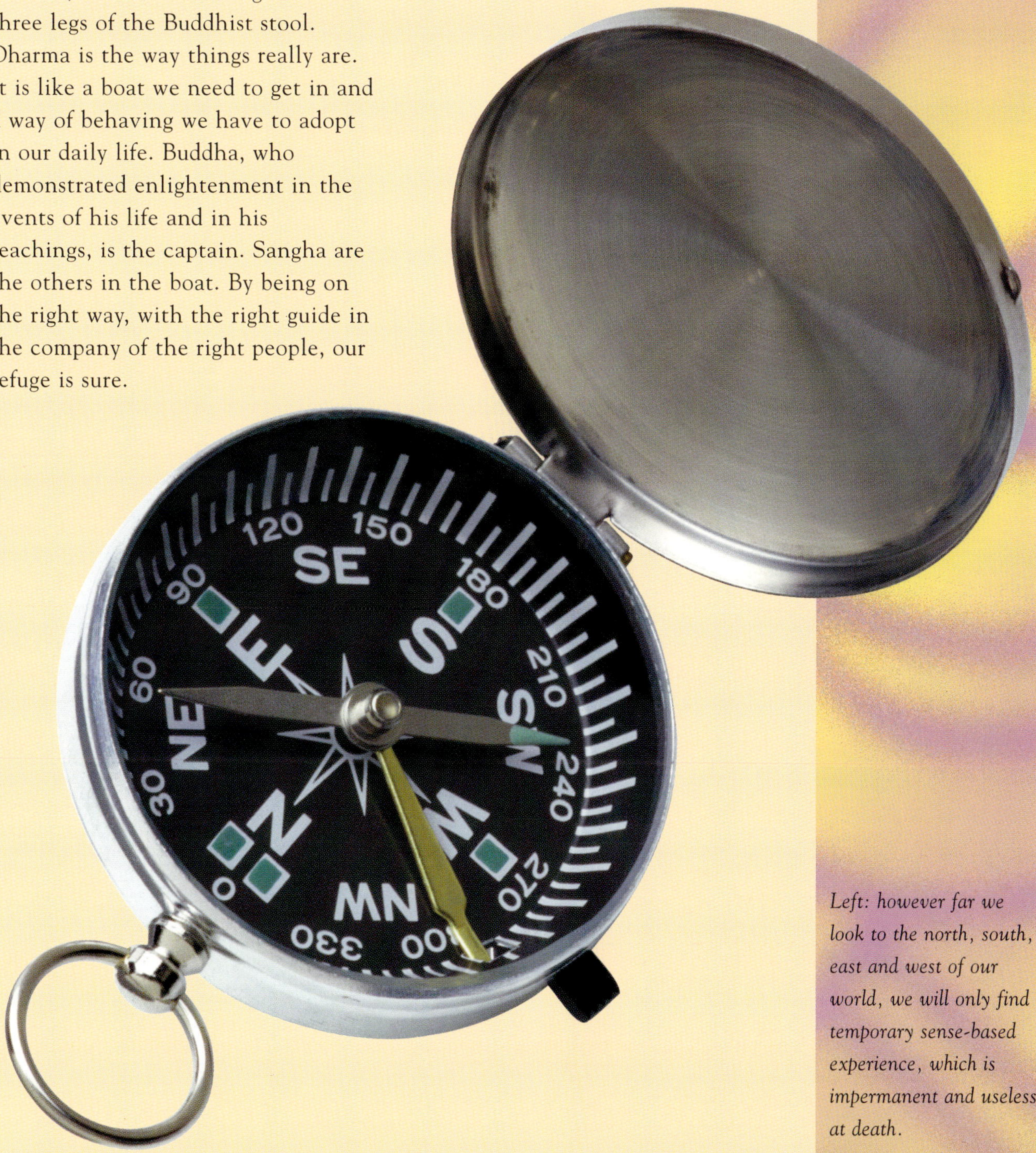

Left: however far we look to the north, south, east and west of our world, we will only find temporary sense-based experience, which is impermanent and useless at death.

Right: when we take refuge in Buddha, we become mindful of the consequences of our actions and, every second of our lives, try to focus on a path of non-harming.

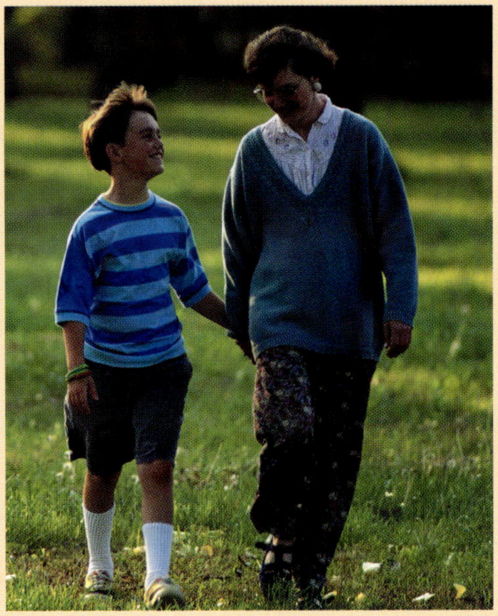

"But what does all this mean in practice? What do we have to do to become a Buddhist and in what practical ways would our lives change, if we did?" At the heart of Buddhism is the commitment not to harm anything in any way – be it by thought, word, or deed. When we take refuge, we commit ourselves to five precepts, or vows. These are to avoid killing, stealing, lying, sexual misconduct and abuse of intoxicants, which are the root causes of all the harm we do. In the previous chapter we learned how by harming others, we create greed, ignorance and hatred. It is this that leads to negative Karma, which confuses our minds and causes our suffering.

When we take refuge in Buddha, we become mindful of the consequences of our actions and, every second of our lives, try to focus on a path of non-harming. Without realising in the past, we were constantly killing animals, insects, microbes, taking what we had not earned, distorting situations and turning them to our advantage, or we were encouraging others to do these things. So now, we try not to walk on insects and harm animals. Every time we eat, we dedicate the energy the food gives us. May the animal that has been killed, or those insects and other animals, which have died, or had their homes destroyed to produce the vegetables not have done so in vain. May the energy we have gained from our food benefit many sentient beings. When we are given the wrong change or find something that is not ours, we give it back. We watch our words, do not deceive and manipulate. We try not to take advantage of other people's misunderstandings.

The commitment regarding sexual misconduct is also very important. Most Buddhist monks interpret this as a vow of celibacy, but there is an important teaching in this vow for sexually active lay people too. The latter engage in sexual misconduct, when they use others solely for personal gratification, without regard to the other's feelings, or interests. Although some actions by their very nature cannot help being abusive of others, generally it is not so much what you do, or who you do it with, as what it does to other people and your own mind that is important. Good sex relieves suffering and creates an expansion of happiness for everyone. Intoxicants are the source of much ignorance, which can lead to harming others and an expansion of suffering. "The morning after the night before", unwanted pregnancies, violence, misunderstandings, revenge, gang fighting, destruction of property, fear, prison, family break-ups, abandoned and abused children, bankruptcy, illness and mindless death – all these sufferings are very likely to have abuse of intoxicants at their core. The dangers are so great and the advantages so few that many Buddhists forego all intoxicants. In certain day-to-day situations, some intoxicants can relieve social tension and clarify the way around blockages briefly, but they cannot be depended upon. If they are used, it should be with great care. Meditation would be more effective.

In all this, we remember the three levels of creating negativity: thinking about doing it; doing it; celebrating the action. We try not to complete this process and, whenever we act wrongly, we purify by recognising, regretting and putting right what we did.

Below: the commitment regarding sexual misconduct is also very important. Most Buddhist monks interpret this as a vow of celibacy, but there is an important teaching in this vow for sexually active lay people too.

Below: in a world where others do follow the precepts, we experience the "coming home" joy of being in the company of "people of good family".

"How can all this be achievable? Do not the 'law of the jungle' and the 'survival of the fittest' mean we have to kill to live and, if everyone else is stealing and lying, we will lose out every time, if we do not join in –

occasionally at least. How can Buddhists keep such vows – they have to be hypocrites?" To think or talk like this is to miss how Karma works. The basic point the Buddha is making is that by living in samsara, we cannot avoid creating negative Karma. This is why we suffer. Hypocrisy does not come into it. Rather, by taking refuge, we start to become more and more mindful and do less and less harm. In short, we create a chain reaction of decency and trust that allows everyone to relax and have confidence in each other and the world they live in. Once again, "the proof of the pudding is in the eating". Those of us who have taken refuge in Buddha, Dharma and Sangha find ourselves in a world that is non-judgmental, where we are encouraged to check up constantly and progress as quickly as we can. This world does not lay a "guilt trip" on us. Rather out of pure compassion, it is keen to see us make progress for our own sake, but cares for and respects us whatever we do. Best of all, after taking refuge and starting on this path, for the first time in our lives we feel we know where we stand and what to do in all situations. Even in a world where others do not follow the precepts, we feel much safer. Because we will not harm others, there is less chance they will harm us. In a world where others do follow the precepts, we experience the "coming home" joy of being in the company of "people of good family".

Whatever happens, we find ourselves laughing!

"In our world today everyone is looking for personal happiness. So, I always say, if you wish to be happy and aim for self-interest, then care for other people. This brings lasting happiness. This is real self-interest, enlightened self-interest."

HH The Dalai Lama of Tibet

Below: to begin visualisation meditation sit comfortably on a chair or on the floor, imagine all sentient beings facing you and your greatest friend coming to the front of them all.

It would be helpful to start this chapter with a reflection, or visualisation meditation, as a Tibetan Buddhist would call it.

As you sit comfortably on a chair or on the floor, imagine all sentient beings facing you and your greatest friend coming to the front of them all. Look at your friend. Try to remember the times you have spent together. Re-live them in your mind. Now consider whether during those times your friend has done things that have caused you harm. Then let the memories fade away completely. Now imagine all sentient beings facing you and a person you do not like, your enemy coming to the front of them all. Look at your enemy for some time. Try to see every detail of his body and bearing. Remember the things that have made him your enemy. Now consider if there have been times when things this enemy did actually led to benefits in your life. Then, let that memory fade away completely.

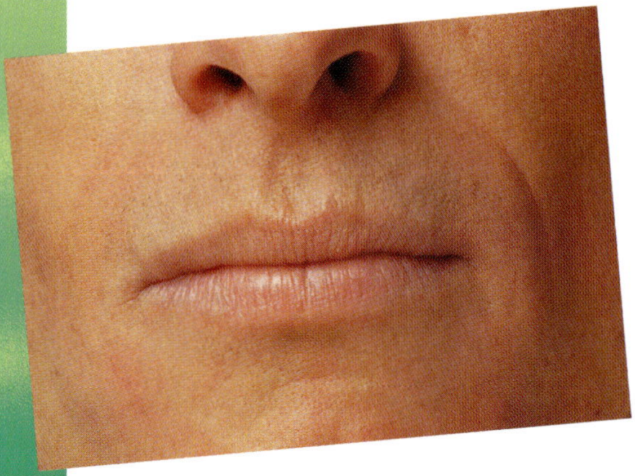

Now imagine all sentient beings facing you and a person you have never seen before coming to the front of them all. Is this stranger your friend or enemy? Should you welcome, reject, or ignore him? Is it more correct to say that there are no friends, enemies and strangers; that the role each person plays in our lives changes from day to day? Most of our problems come from labelling others as friends, enemies and strangers and treating them accordingly.

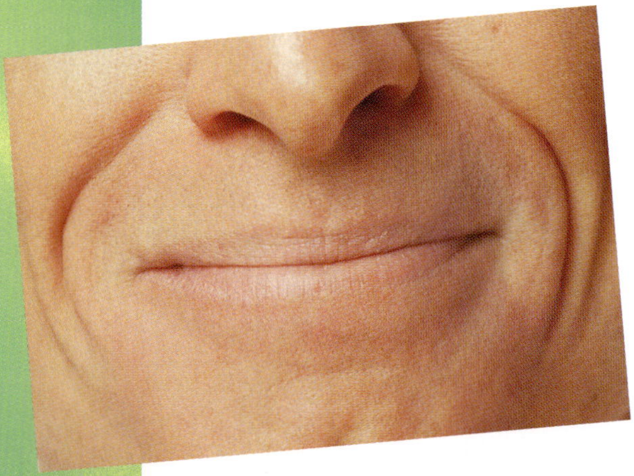

This blocks understanding, opportunity and progress in our lives. So there is no reason to be attached to and give special help to a friend, or return harm to an enemy.

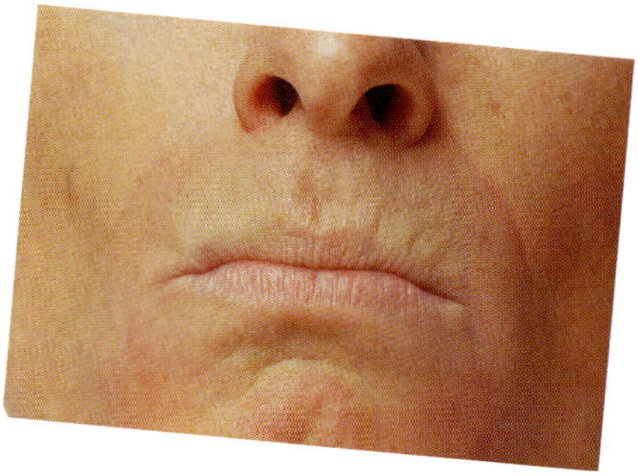

Tibetan Buddhists take this meditation one stage further. They visualise how various beings have been their friend in one lifetime, enemy in another and stranger in a third over and over again. So, throughout beginningless time, relative labelling of the same beings into friend, enemy and stranger has created problems. This labelling is self-grasping ignorance, which leads to greedy attachment to our own possessive "happiness", which of course is not happiness at all. These delusions have caused all the hatred, harm and dangers in our own and everyone else's myriad lifetimes.

This is not to deny that some people can behave very badly towards us. Of course they can, but to assume we are the judge of their behaviour and the consequences of their actions may be to miss the truth altogether. A Tibetan lama was being driven to the airport on a crowded road when a car overtook and cut in front in an extremely dangerous way. "The fool – he could have killed us all", the lama's driver found himself saying. "He is your kind Buddha teacher", said the lama gently almost under his breath. Immediately, the tension was eased not only for that journey, but for all "road rage" situations that driver found himself in in the future. Afflictions are in our own mind.

Our deluded minds draw situations towards us ideally suited to exacerbate these delusions. The more difficult or unreasonable the situation, the more useful it is to develop a crucial mind state of equanimity. With equanimity problems will be solved and fade into dust. With equanimity in our minds, we see things clearly and so can care for the most difficult people, even should they rise against us. The enemy is just the conception of our hate, just as friend and stranger are conceived by our greed and ignorance.

Below: the more difficult or unreasonable the situation, the more useful it is to develop a crucial mind state of equanimity.

Above: crucially, throughout beginningless time there have always been numberless mothers.

With this understanding of equanimity in our minds, we can consider the most important concept of Mahayana Buddhism – Bodhicitta.

> *"If we divided this earth into pieces the size of juniper berries,*
> *The number of these would not be as great*
> *As the number of times that*
> *Each sentient being has been our mother."*
>
> *Nagarjuna*

Because mind is beginningless, but samsara has not ended, reincarnation has always existed. Hence my previous lives are infinite in number. So, I have experienced every kind of lifetime, as a human, an ant, an elephant, a flea and so on. So my mother of this lifetime has been my mother of many other lifetimes in all kinds of forms. Not always of course. At times the roles were reversed, or we had no contact at all. She or we may have been someone else's mothers. Crucially, throughout beginningless time there have always been numberless mothers.

We are all grateful for the kindness of our present mothers from conception to death. They give birth and nurture us. They provide the body that has the senses, through which all sensual enjoyment emanates – everything we touch, taste, smell, see and hear. Mothers give us the flesh of their bodies. They clean, feed, cloth, shelter and educate us. Many would even die for their offspring.

Left: we are all grateful for the kindness of our present mothers from conception to death. They give birth and nurture us.

Far left: Lama Karma, Kalachakra, Jispa, 1994.

The most natural thing in the world is to feel gratitude for the selfless kindness of our own mothers and to admire the selfless kindness of all the mothers of all creatures, throughout all time. From this gratitude comes a wish to repay the great kindness by developing compassion, the compassion of the mother, not just for people close to us, but for all sentient (sense-based) beings.

This becomes easy, when we realise that throughout beginningless time, every sentient being has been our mother countless times and we have been their mothers. So, we should repay them with the same kindness, as we would wish to repay our mother in this lifetime for her kindness. This profound wish to be kind is called Bodhicitta. It is the heart quality of the Bodhisattva, who dedicates his life to effortless and total compassion to benefit all sentient beings without exception.

Developing the compassion of Bodhicitta is the essential way that the Mahayana Buddhist becomes enlightened. He does this by realising there is no real separation between himself and others. Indeed, the Bodhisattva makes the commitment that he will not become enlightened, until all other sentient beings are enlightened. All benefits he receives, all his achievements and merits for his kindness, he will dedicate to others in a way that will serve their achieving enlightenment. He sees no separation between himself and others and so will take on the suffering of all sentient beings.

Above: 1,000 Armed Chenresig.

Stories of the Buddha's previous lives as a Bodhisattva illustrate this very well. One day he came across a lioness starving and unable to feed her young. He was so full of compassion that he cut his own body and offered her the blood for nourishment. Moved by great compassion, the Buddha vowed that he wished his body to be split into a thousand pieces should he in any lifetime cease to serve all sentient beings absolutely. One day, he was confronted by the most evil man of that time. "If you are such a great Bodhisattva, who can give his body to benefit others, why not give me your arm?" Calmly the Buddha took a knife and cut off and offered his right arm only to have it thrown back in his face. "How dare you offer me anything with your filthy left hand!" was the exclamation. At which the Buddha found himself say, "How can one ever care for all sentient beings, when...". Before he had finished speaking, his body split into a thousand pieces, but froze in the process as he became enlightened. He now understood fully what is involved in being a fully realised Bodhisattva, dedicated to the release from samsara and happiness of all sentient beings.

With this story we see the crucial link between Mahayana Buddhism and Christ's Crucifixion. It brings us to the deepest truth of oneness and compassion between all beings that lies at the very heart of existence.

"How wonderful it would be if all sentient beings were to abide in equanimity free of hatred and attachment!
May they always abide in equanimity free of hatred and attachment!
I myself will cause them to abide in equanimity free of hatred and attachment!
Please Guru Buddha grant me blessings to be able to do this!

How wonderful it would be if all sentient beings had happiness and its causes!
May they always have happiness and its causes!
I myself will cause them to have happiness and its causes!
Please Guru Buddha grant me blessings to be able to do this!

How wonderful it would be if all sentient beings were free of suffering and its causes!
May they always be free of suffering and its causes!
I myself will cause them to be free of suffering and its causes!
Please Guru Buddha grant me blessings to be able to do this!

How wonderful it would be if all sentient beings were never separated from the happiness of higher rebirth and liberation!
May they never be separated from the happiness of higher rebirth and liberation!
I myself will cause them never to be separated from the happiness of higher rebirth and liberation!
Please Guru Buddha grant me blessings to be able to do this!"

Traditional Prayer

Driven determinedly by the irresistible, compassionate motivation of Bodhicitta, the Bodhisattva seeks by every means to ensure success in caring for others. All his endeavours can be crystallised into six groups of perfect actions. The fifth – concentration – and sixth – emptiness – are considered in the next two chapters. This leaves the first four to this chapter. These are generosity, morality, patience and enthusiasm or perseverance.

Below: generosity, morality, patience and enthusiasm or perseverance are four of the six groups of perfect actions.

Visualise the openhearted spirit of Christmas giving, without the exploitative commercialism and nagging sense of obligation that can so easily degenerate into over-indulged resentment. Pure giving without any of these negativities is the nature of the perfection of generosity. We give for its own sake, because we want to give. We imagine a constant expansion of giving. Tibetans offer water at their daily morning *puja*. In their mountains it is plentiful and easy to give without attachment. This develops a mindset of unhindered generosity. We try to identify with the recipient of our giving. This ensures everything offered is exactly appropriate. It will bring happiness and not harm. In spite of all this care we take, there are no grudging conditions.

Maybe we give exactly the right thing, but the recipient does not understand, or appreciate our generosity. We continue to give with the same enthusiasm, seeking to increase our skill and focus. We have no expectations for ourselves. For the Bodhisattva all giving is holy, offered on an altar for a higher purpose, given completely, without a single thought of a reward, or miserliness.

Above: visualise the openhearted spirit of Christmas giving, without the exploitative commercialism and nagging sense of obligation.

Far left: monks receiving bread; a Monlam prayer festival, Jokhang Temple, Lhasa, central Tibet.

Below: in our heart of hearts we all know the difference between right and wrong. "You cannot hide it from your conscience, or "lie to God", as Christians put it. There is no lawyer, who can "get us off the hook" of knowing we have been dishonest, or immoral.

In seeking to repay others' kindness towards us, being honest and decent toward them is always is an invaluable gift. In our heart of hearts we all know the difference between right and wrong. "We cannot hide it from our conscience, or "lie to God", as Christians put it. There is no lawyer, who can "get us off the hook" of knowing we have been dishonest, or immoral. So, if we wish to care for others, let us behave as though "God is watching" all the time. Nor should we use the immoral behaviour of others as an excuse. To behave badly in return helps no one. If we continue with our moral behaviour, we must succeed in the end. There is no other way. We should be keen to act morally, full of hope, focused exactly on encouraging the maximum decency in the most number of people. Yet, we seek no recognition. Success and enlightenment is achieved, when everyone is living happily in a moral world. Knowing how this came about is only important if it helps bring future happiness. The bringer of happiness should not seek a reward. There can be no greater reward than the clarity of knowing we all are and always have been of the same mind.

In rich contemporary societies, we live in the midst of plenty, yet "road rage" and many other attacks and feelings of retribution are on the increase. In contrast, war and hardship seem to bring out the best in people. When the situation is clear and options are limited, we develop patience and get on with the task in hand. This brings us happiness and friendship. Knowing Shantideva's words that "wholesome deeds ... amassed over a thousand aeons, will be destroyed in one moment of anger", the Bodhisattva seeks out and welcomes every opportunity to practice patience. We should not blame and punish others for acting angrily towards us. Their behaviour is caused by their anger. To punish them would be as pointless as punishing a stick that someone hits us with. The angrier we get with heat and cold, wind and rain, sickness and beatings, the more harm they will cause us. The more we are patient in these and all situations; the clearer will be our minds and hence the more appropriate and successful our actions. A western tourist complained to a Tibetan doctor about the fleas in her bedroom. She was given medicine to ease her nerves. Of four people in a room, the only one being bitten by mosquitoes was the one trying to swat them! By being patient, we ease tension and suffering, and clear blockages and misunderstandings. We create an environment, where barriers break down, other views are understood and a happier, more mutually supportive society is created.

Left: the angrier we get with heat and cold, wind and rain, sickness and beatings, the more harm they will cause us.

Above: we take labour-saving devices for granted. They are made in factories by other labour-saving machine tools, driven by computers and programmed in advance to repeat production procedures with the minimum of human intervention.

We take labour-saving devices for granted. They are made in factories by other labour-saving machine tools, driven by computers and programmed in advance to repeat production procedures with the minimum of human intervention. Now we are trying to develop artificial intelligence, so the computer will be able to work out how to instruct and manufacture machines without our help. None of this is wrong in itself, unless it encourages Shantideva's "pleasurable taste of idleness" that degenerates into a state of mindless ignorance. We "get stoned and we miss it", or, as Harry Enfield put it in *The Slobs*, "I cannot be asked to do that!" In contrast, the Bodhisattva is constantly keen to act to help others. Realising that death might come at any second, he is reluctant to sleep, or become distracted by frivolous amusements. What greater satisfaction can there be than constantly wishing to increase happiness by helping others? Then we dedicate these merits to further helping others in a continuous stream of service. Nor do we count the cost to ourselves of all our efforts. We are always on hand, generous, appropriate, patient and persistent – doing all we can to act to open doors to enlightenment.

"Surely, these four perfect actions of the Bodhisattva are far too idealist and unrealistic. We are bound to fall short as soon as we start?" Such a reservation is a defeatist recipe for eternal pessimism. If adopting these four perfect actions is crucial to our happiness, what else is there to do, but start on this path that will train, cleanse and enlighten our minds? Just by making a commitment to try will make our minds feel clearer and happier. For many people it brings a sense of being safe and at home at last.

The 20th century saw us: fighting and threatening to fight bloody wars; creating comfortable consumer societies; developing legal systems to protect, punish and compensate; financing social welfare and health systems to take care of the needy. Yet, this has left most of us more demanding and desperate for a system of values that will give sense and purpose to the world we live in. The rigidity of traditional values, the laissez-faire of the sexual revolution, capitalism, soviet socialism, rock and roll, modern scientific developments, even football only separate us from each other and the happiness we seek. Not that we are without hope. There have been moments when people seemed to let go of personal prejudices and come together. Usually this has been at times of natural disasters, famines, genocide, or the death of an individual who has inspired mass compassion.

Below: the 20th century saw us: fighting and threatening to fight bloody wars; creating comfortable consumer societies; developing legal systems to protect, punish and compensate.

Above: well-intentioned laws and political decisions, based on prejudiced sympathy, rather than compassion for all, have caused much suffering. The more we seek to label and act to condemn and punish, the more we build up problems for everyone.

Nothing inspires and unifies more than the opening of the heart in compassion toward others. When it happens we have to be careful. Such mass displays can be dangerous, when they are channelled in to mass hysteria and religious prejudice. Then the best of intentions can lead to mindless persecution and religious and racial intolerance. Well-intentioned laws and political decisions, based on prejudiced sympathy, rather than compassion for all, have caused much suffering. The more we seek to label and act to condemn and punish, the more we build up problems for everyone, be it the criminal or his victim. Indeed it is this modern tendency to believe we can legislate and decide policy that "deals with wrongdoing for good" that is unrealistic and doomed to failure.

In contrast, the perfections of generosity, morality, patience and enthusiasm, when given to all without fear or favour, can dismantle barriers and open hearts. They can bring an understanding and tolerance that will start a trend towards making our societies safer and pleasanter to live in. The more of us that learn how to do this as we move through life, the more happiness will be seen and exchanged between us. If we wish to cover the whole world with leather, this would be impossible, but by wearing just one pair of shoes, or sandals, we create the same effect.

Of course, we will need clear direction and hard realism to strengthen these four ideal practices. To establish a sure focus and firm foundation for this path of the Bodhisattva, the next two chapters will consider the fifth and sixth perfections – concentration and emptiness.

Below: the perfections of generosity, morality, patience and enthusiasm, when given to all without fear or favour, can dismantle barriers and open hearts.

Far right: Thangka of Sakyamuni Buddha, Ki Monastery, Spiti, India.

Below: large white Buddha statue near the Ambasthale Dagoba, Mihinitale, Sri Lanka.

"Those who wish to destroy the many sorrows
Of (their) conditioned existence,
Those, who wish (all beings) to experience a multitude of joys,
And those who wish to experience much happiness,
Should never forsake the awakening mind.

It is like a supreme gold-making elixir,
For it transforms the unclean body we have taken
Into the priceless jewel of a Buddha-form.
Therefore firmly seize this awakening mind."

Shantideva

Until we try meditating, few of us realise there is anything strange and dysfunctional about the way most of our minds work. We do not notice the constant buzz of thoughts, with their expectations, fears, hopes, resentments, imaginations and so on. It is the uncontrolled negativity in our minds that causes so much suffering for others and ourselves. To realise we are at the mercy of our thoughts is the first liberation that meditation offers. To accept that it will take a bit of time to change this, but it will be most beneficial to take this first step of observing what is going on is the second liberation.

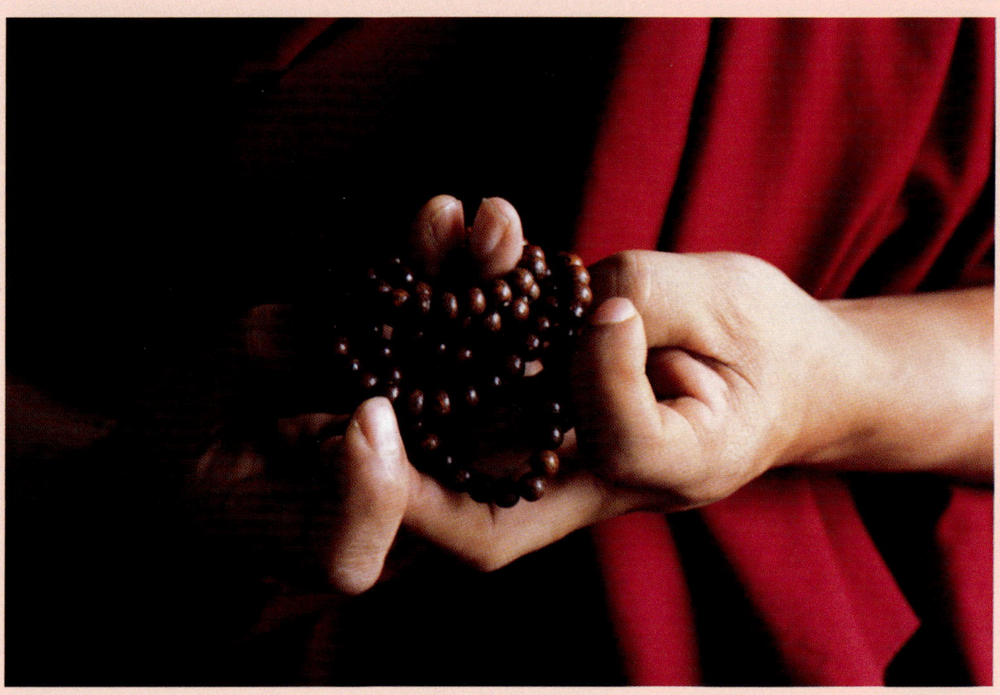

Right: the fingers of your right hand should be facing up and resting on the fingers of the left one with the thumbs gently touching. The circle this makes should be around your navel.

Far right: until we try meditating, few of us realise there is anything strange and dysfunctional about the way most of our minds work.

So, set a time limit – maybe fifteen minutes for the first time; half an hour or longer, when you feel ready. Maybe set a gentle watch alarm, if you are doing this on your own. Then you will not be concerned with the time. It is better to meditate on an empty stomach. There is less chance of drowsiness, or discomfort, which leads to distraction. First thing in the morning is the best time. In the evening, before dinner is also good, if you can find the time. Just before you go to bed at night is very valuable.

The first step is to neutralise the way the body dominates our lives and hence our mind. So, focus on posture. Ideally, sit cross-legged on a carpeted floor with a firm, but comfortable cushion under the base of the posterior. Let the legs be comfortably folded – very few people can achieve a full, or even half lotus. Although if either of these comes naturally, the position is far more balanced. The crucial thing is to keep the back straight, but not too tight, nor too loose. The former will craze and distract the mind; the latter induces sleep. So experiment between tightness and looseness until a comfortable middle way is found.

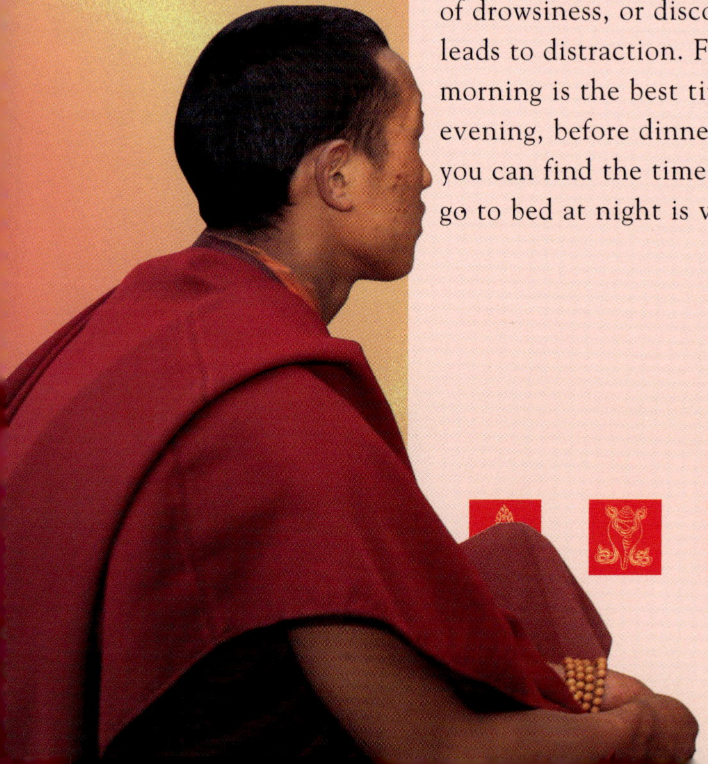

Visualise a saucer of light resting gently on the crown of your head and that it descends slowly downwards in and around your body. Every part of the body this touches it relaxes in to the middle way. As you imagine the saucer descending, with your inner eye try to ensure all your muscles relax to this middle way. Check that: your eyes are lightly nearly shut, not closed tight; that your teeth are slightly apart, not clenched; the tip of your tongue touches the roof of your upper palate; your lips are gently closed; your head is resting just a little forward and comfortably on your shoulders; your back is not rigid, but naturally supporting your body. The fingers of your right hand should be facing up and resting on the fingers of the left one with the thumbs gently touching. The circle this makes should be around your navel. Again ensure your legs are crossed and comfortable and your body now ready to be still. If you can, try not to move, but do not fight it. If you have to, move once then be still. To fidget disturbs the mind. If you are unable to sit on the floor, try to adopt a balanced posture, while sitting in an upright chair. It is best to avoid lying down. It can dull the mind.

Right: monks at Sera Monastery, Tibet.

Far right: let your inner mind focus on the breath. This is all there is to do. The body does not move, nor should the mind. Just focus on the breath coming in and out of your body.

From this physical stillness let your inner mind focus on the breath. This is all there is to do. The body does not move, nor should the mind. Just focus on the breath coming in and out of your body. "Watch" it carefully – in and out, in and out – just keep on watching it. If thoughts come, do not welcome, regret, fight or hold on to them in any other way. See them as clouds in the sky. Note how they change and are as insubstantial as those clouds. Do not let them dominate your mind with their imagined importance. You will remember to "get the vegetables", to "phone John or Mary", to "put that idea in your book", "remind Charlie about your promotion" etc. etc. Just return to the breath as it goes in and out. Let the body rest motionless in neutral – just concentrate on the breath.

It might help to count your breaths – one in and out, two in and out and so on. See if you can reach 21, without becoming distracted. Be especially careful of the distraction of congratulating yourself on reaching 15 breaths! Do not try too hard, or struggle with guilt and failure – observe everything from outside it. Do not hang on to whatever you are thinking.

Rest upon your breath. Visualise it coming in through your right nostril, filling your lungs, and then let it pass out through your left nostril. Try to do this 21 times. Then rest, just breathing for a while. Now try to reach 21 again. All the time, let thoughts come and go – do not hang on to them.

Right: as you hear the signal to end the meditation, sit gently for a while longer. It is good at this time not to worry how well you have or have not done, but rather to hope any benefits will help as many people as possible.

As you hear the signal to end the meditation, sit gently for a while longer. It is good at this time not to worry how well you have or have not done, but rather to hope any benefits will help as many people as possible. Then you move back into action naturally and continue with your normal life. However it went, nearly everyone finds the experience therapeutic. Even if your thoughts bombarded you without ceasing, at least you now know this is the condition of your mind. It can be a vital first step. For next time you are consumed with anxiety, or expectation, you will find it easier to handle. Most people find they are performing everyday tasks more smoothly and spontaneously, because there is less mental anxiety. Everyone gains from that.

Having developed a technique that suits, the best way to progress is to meditate regularly – every morning and in the evening if possible. Again, do not punish yourself with a tight schedule and guilt about not keeping to it. Just check up whether you feel better, when you keep to a regular meditation schedule.

Of course, this is just a first, albeit incredibly important, technique. The Tibetans have hundreds of others. No one could practise them all. Below are a couple more you may wish to try.

As well as focusing on the breath, it can sometimes help to focus on another object. Tibetan cymbals have a particular resonance that can hold the mind clear of other distractions. You sound them by allowing them to crash together, then holding them suspended until the sound completely fades. The problem is making this sound without becoming distracted by the practicalities! Maybe you could incorporate the logistics into your sitting posture. If you have a tape recorder, then you could record the sound at regular intervals, or you could meditate with a friend and take turns. The crucial thing is to let the mind rest on and beyond the sound and the steady in and out movement of the breath. Remember, there is nothing else that is more important, than the breath. While we breathe we live – nothing else is so vital.

Below: a Tibetan monk with symbols.

Developing this single-pointed concentration will become the foundation of everything we think and do. We can further develop it to train our minds to practise the compassionate care of Bodhicitta for all other sentient beings. When you are ready to try this, adopt your usual posture and do some breathing meditation, bringing yourself to focus on the entry of the breath in through the right-hand nostril and out through the left-hand one. Now imagine around you every person and creature caught up and suffering in sense-dependent existence – all sentient beings. You may find it easier at first to concentrate on people dear to your heart, for instance mother, father, partner, children, friends and relatives. Now try to be aware of their sickness, hardships, emotional problems and things that confuse them. As you breathe in through your right nostril imagine all these sufferings entering you in the form of a dark fog, which concentrates into a hard black rock. This explodes within you into lightning, which shatters the hard black rock of delusion into myriad tiny pieces.

Right: when practising the compassionate care of Bodhicitta for all other sentient beings you may find it easier at first to concentrate on people dear to your heart, for instance mother, father, partner, children, friends and relatives.

Far right: His Holiness the Dalai Lama (left)

These pieces disappear into nothingness. Then as you breathe out through your left nostril, imagine yourself sending out pure white light from your own and Buddha's holy body to every sentient being that surrounds you. Every atom of this white light causes great happiness and cures the sufferings, fear and distress of all sentient beings. Then repeat this visualisation as many times as you wish. At the end be pleased that all the sufferings have been cleared forever, definitely.

As you leave the meditation in your usual way, dedicate all the merits that have been gained from this visualisation, so that every sentient being, those you do know and those you do not know, may experience the happiness of pure Buddha mind.

"Form is emptiness; emptiness is form. Emptiness is not other than form; form also is not other than emptiness. Likewise, feeling, discrimination, compositional factors and consciousness are empty. Shariputra, like this all phenomena are merely empty, having no characteristics. They are not produced and do not cease. They have no defilement and no separation from defilement. They have no decrease and increase.

"Therefore, Shariputra, in emptiness there is no form, no feeling, no discrimination, no compositional factors, no consciousness. There is no eye, no ear, no nose, no tongue, no body, no mind; no form no sound, no smell, no taste, no tactile object, no phenomenon. There is no eye element and so forth, up to no mind element, and also up to no element of mental consciousness. There is no ignorance and no exhaustion of ignorance, and so forth up to no ageing and death and no exhaustion of ageing and death. Likewise, there is no suffering, origin, cessation or path; no exalted wisdom, no attainment and also no non-attainment.

"Therefore, Shariputra, because there is no attainment, all bodhisattvas rely on and abide in the perfection of wisdom; their minds have no obstructions and no fear. Passing utterly beyond perversity, they attain the final state beyond sorrow. Also, all the buddhas who perfectly reside in the three times, relying upon the perfection of wisdom, become manifest and complete buddhas in the state of unsurpassed, perfect and complete enlightenment."

The Heart Sutra

Many of the main concepts, quotations and examples in this book so far have been drawn from a carefully structured teaching, brought to Tibet by Atisha in the second half of the first millennium AD. It is called *Lam Rim – The Graduated Path to Enlightenment.*

To teach all the main elements, with associated meditations to develop realisation, can take many days, weeks – even months. At the last session of one such month-long teaching of the *Lam Rim Chen Mo* (Chen Mo means longer, greater), the lama reached the topic of Ultimate Truth – Emptiness. In dry, neutral and deceptively intellectual tones, he outlined the main ideas from the Heart Sutra quoted above. Then he stopped speaking, looked up at the packed meditation hall, smiled and said gently, "Any questions?" "Yes," boomed a loud voice from the back, "if the final teaching is about this emptiness and you are saying there are no senses, body, path, or anything, then what about this Buddha then (pointing to the large statue beside the lama). Does he exist?" All eyes turned to the lama, whose faced eased into a broad grin as he gently shook his head from side to side. Spontaneously, the hall broke into a relieving laughter of reassured understanding.

Below: Buddhist monks debating the teachings; an afternoon ritual at Sera Monastery, Lhasa, Tibet.

The teachings of the Buddha are full of profound paradoxes, but none is more fundamental than Wisdom – the Ultimate Truth of Emptiness. Full of pictures, paintings, sounds, colours, holy texts dedicated to holy deities though it is, when you get to Buddhism's heart there is a very special kind of emptiness. Not that it is really empty. Here comes the enlightening final paradox. How can emptiness be empty, unless it is empty of its own emptiness? If it were not, it would be full of emptiness, not empty.

While there is emptiness as opposed to fullness, we have only relative truth. To label something as perfect, we must have labels of imperfect. Good needs evil, "God" needs the devil and so on. As soon as we take refuge in something that is dependent on something else, we take a prejudiced view and do not see clearly. For this reason, you cannot take refuge in there being no thing – claiming that nihilism is the ultimate truth. This indeed is dangerous delusion. There are rules, but they are the rules of relative existence. The law of Karma is an exactly accurate description of the way that delusion works in the relative world of samsara. When karma is cleared, we move beyond. Then we understand the ultimate truth of emptiness, which is empty of its own emptiness.

This apparently obscure philosophising is not irrelevant nit-picking and playing on words for the sake of doing so. It has vitally important implications for every decision and action every one of us takes. The ignorance and hatred that causes our suffering comes from our judging what happens, as if it has an absolute cause, when it really has a relative one. "That person has never liked me." "You have always loved my elder brother more than me." "Labour politicians are hypocrites." "They are prejudiced against this that or other type of person." "A Christian would not behave like that." Crusades have been fought, Jerusalem is divided, and attempts are made to wipe out whole races of people all because of deluded views of what is "absolute truth".

Far left: pilgrims watching a prayer service as part of a Monlam prayer festival, Labrang Monastery, Amdo, Eastern Tibet.

Below: when we start training our minds to remember that anything that happens is empty of absolute nature we find ourselves still existing and far happier in this ultimately empty universe.

In contrast, when we start training our minds to remember that anything that happens is empty of absolute nature, we put aside attachment to what we feel is most precious. This leaves our minds free to develop compassion and to see things as they really are. And, most amazing of all, we find ourselves still existing and far happier in this ultimately empty universe. Because it is empty of its own emptiness. It is eternal, beginningless mind.

When we get to the heart of it, this Buddhist concept of emptiness is not different to the essential mystical truth at the heart of all the main world religions. Christ's crucifixion for our sins is very similar to Chenrezig's realisation at the end of Chapter 5. In essence, the mystical omnipresent God, both within and without every one of us, which is the ultimate truth of Christianity, Judaism, Islam and Hinduism, is little different to the Buddhist wisdom of emptiness. Problems occur when a religious group personalise and become attached to their relationship with the deity – when they treat the relative as if it were an absolute thing. Then they can exclude others, who they see as having a different, "improper" relationship. "Christ may have died for all sinners, but, if you do not accept him as I do, you cannot be redeemed." "I know the truth. You do not", may be so, but it is not for one person or another to decide what is or is not absolute. When we open ourselves out to being found by the truth, we may know it. When we stand up for "the truth" against all others, self-righteous fanaticism leading to great suffering is much more likely.

This sixth perfection of the Ultimate Truth of Emptiness, or Sunyata, is crucial to the safety of all Buddhist spiritual practice. Bringing our minds back to the Heart Sutra dispels the erupting pride of self-importance. It makes it easier to dedicate everything we do to others. It makes us more accepting and acceptable, less fanatical, more healing. To keep the practice clear and clean, Tibetan monks love to debate the philosophical details of Sunyata with stylised dramatic physical movements. Here is an example from Shantideva *Guide to the Bodhisattva's Way of Life*:

"Question – But isn't the mind of the present (moment) which has been produced but has not yet ceased, the self?

Answer – If this were the case, then in the next moment, when it had perished, it would no longer be the self.

Question – If there were no sentient being, towards whom could compassion be developed?

Answer – Although sentient beings do not truly exist, deceptively one should develop compassion for those imputed as sentient beings by the confused mind which has promised to practise the (Bodhisattva) way of life in order to lead them to the goal of liberation."

Below: monks debating.

Below: we live in a world of uncertain values, conflicting loyalties and unbridled technological innovation, dominated by "expert" material scientists.

Such uncompromising questioning of the very heart techniques of Dharma practice keeps it calm and strong. Buddhists do not have a faith to question; they have practice that they use, if they find it beneficial. Within the implications of their Ultimate Truth of Emptiness lie paradoxes of ever-stronger understanding and reassurance that cannot be described in words.

We live in a world of uncertain values, conflicting loyalties and unbridled technological innovation, dominated by "expert" material scientists. Modern physics now tells us that black holes may well form the centre of every galaxy. The essential quality of a black hole is a dramatic increase of density and gravitational pull. Theoretically, at its centre there is said to be a singularity – that is, a dimensionless object of infinite density. From this, science fiction fantasises that a wormhole may form. We can build machines that transcend the limitations of the speed of light and project us through the wormhole into other universes and times. If this were possible, then this would be another level of relativity. If not, then maybe physical science is looking so far outward that it has seen what Buddhist meditation masters have realised inside for thousands of years.

Discussing the Buddhist view of emptiness is most suitable and beneficial in today's world. We complain there is nothing to believe in, or fight for any more. Day-to-day life and politics are about style and manipulation. We live in an everyone-for-themselves society. Yet, if we look back, it has always been like that. The navies of Elizabeth I, the Spanish and Portuguese were often no more than pirate ships ravishing what was not theirs. Victorian imperial values were attempts to give moral justification to theft and exploitation. Every country's history has similar skeletons in its cupboards. Every expression of aggressive nationalism leads to an expansion of unhappiness.

That relative values, however idealistic and sweet sounding, can bring absolute meaning and happiness is a cruel pretence. Instead, they have caused all the suffering we read about in our history. We know enough today to see this, but turn instead to full-out individual, self-indulgent sensuality to avoid facing what is left – the "terrible truth of emptiness".

Above: discussing the Buddhist view of emptiness is most suitable and beneficial in today's world. We live in an everyone-for-themselves society. Yet, if we look back, it has always been like that.

Above: properly understood, Buddhism's uncompromising view of emptiness is not terrible, but truly wonderful and may well be an extremely relevant foundation to debate the issues of the new millennium..

Yet, properly understood and combined with an absolute dedication of compassion towards all sentient beings, Buddhism's uncompromising view of emptiness is not terrible, but truly wonderful. It offers a cleansing, clarifying and logical view of things as they are. It has meaning for all, be they technically or spiritually minded. Such wisdom may well be an extremely relevant foundation to debate the issues of the new millennium.

ACCELERATING THE PROCESS FOR THE BENEFIT OF OTHERS

The out-of-this-world quality of the thankas, mantras, strange sounding instruments and aromas of Tibetan Buddhism fascinate our 21st-century minds. We sense something beautiful, special and at times frightening, but what does it all mean and how does it fit into the pure idealism of the Buddha's teachings?

Below: monks at a ceremony in the Jokhang Temple, Lhasa, Tibet.

It is this third Vajrayana (or Tantrayana) vehicle that makes Tibetan different to any other form of Buddhism. Tibetan Buddhist tantra transforms normal sensual objects. It orders and dedicates them in such a way that the process of understanding, purifying Karma and hence benefiting others is accelerated. The practitioner is encouraged to focus on idealised archetypes. Cloth, or paper paintings of various forms of the Buddha (known as thankas) are displayed. The layout of these is traditionally passed down from generation to generation – every spatial relationship and object in the picture has a meaning that is written and explained in commentaries. Associated with the thankas are particular ceremonies to heighten and develop realisation within the practitioner. Sometimes a mandala made from coloured sand is constructed with painstaking detail. Central to the ceremony is the repetition of appropriate mantras, or holy phrases. There will also be careful colour attributes, aromas and sounds.

Just to see the picture is considered to be a blessing. In traditional Tibet, lamas would be invited and sponsored to travel around. They would unroll and display their thankas, perform the accompanying puja and encourage people to make contact with its ideal qualities. Many would adorn the walls of temples. To recite the mantra many times brings great benefits to an increasing number of people. The serious student will take an initiation and go deeper in their understanding of the full commentary. This is indeed an enlightening insight into the scholarship and power of the Tibetan tradition.

The various Buddha images displayed on the thankas and invoked in the ceremonies can be seen as idealised psychological archetypes that could form a very valuable part of modern therapy. Chenrezig symbolises compassion. By developing compassion for others, we understand them and so release ourselves from fear and separation. Manjushri's wisdom cuts through delusion. By being clear in our minds, deluded thoughts that lead to misunderstandings and fruitless efforts are removed. Tara is the mother that removes obstacles. Feeling a mother beside us, who will clear away everything preventing the success of our purely motivated efforts, gives us great strength and ensures we lead a moral life.

There are hundreds of Tibetan Buddhist tantric images. They cover the whole spectrum of the human mind and its activities from the most attractive to the most frightening. All are dedicated and presented in a way that has a very accelerating, cleansing effect on our minds and behaviour. They move us to compassion and the motivation to care for others. They protect us against those that do not understand and would harm the way of Dharma. Tibetan Buddhist tantra is the most complete method of therapy. It is suited to all minds in all ages and is especially relevant today.

Above: in traditional Tibet, lamas would be invited and sponsored to travel around. They would unroll and display their thankas, perform the accompanying puja and encourage people to make contact with its ideal qualities.

As with modern allopathic medicine, however, the best cures can be the most dangerous if improperly used. To try to use tantric methods self-interestedly to gain personal power can cause great harm to us and our associates. The egocentric mind constantly imagines terrors and threats from others. To try to gain advantage by invoking, or casting spells causes us to imagine someone else is doing this to us. To seek to gain power over another person by the force of one's mind is to isolate oneself increasingly. Indeed, the worst mental state in the Buddhist teachings is what the Tibetans call Vajra Hell. This state of complete mental paranoia is so totally self-created that it is almost impossible to escape. Obsessive misuse of tantra for the wrong reasons leads us in this direction. We become as much the victims of our own bad mental attitude as do all the villains in literature.

Below: as with modern allopathic medicine, however, the best tantric cures can be the most dangerous if improperly used.

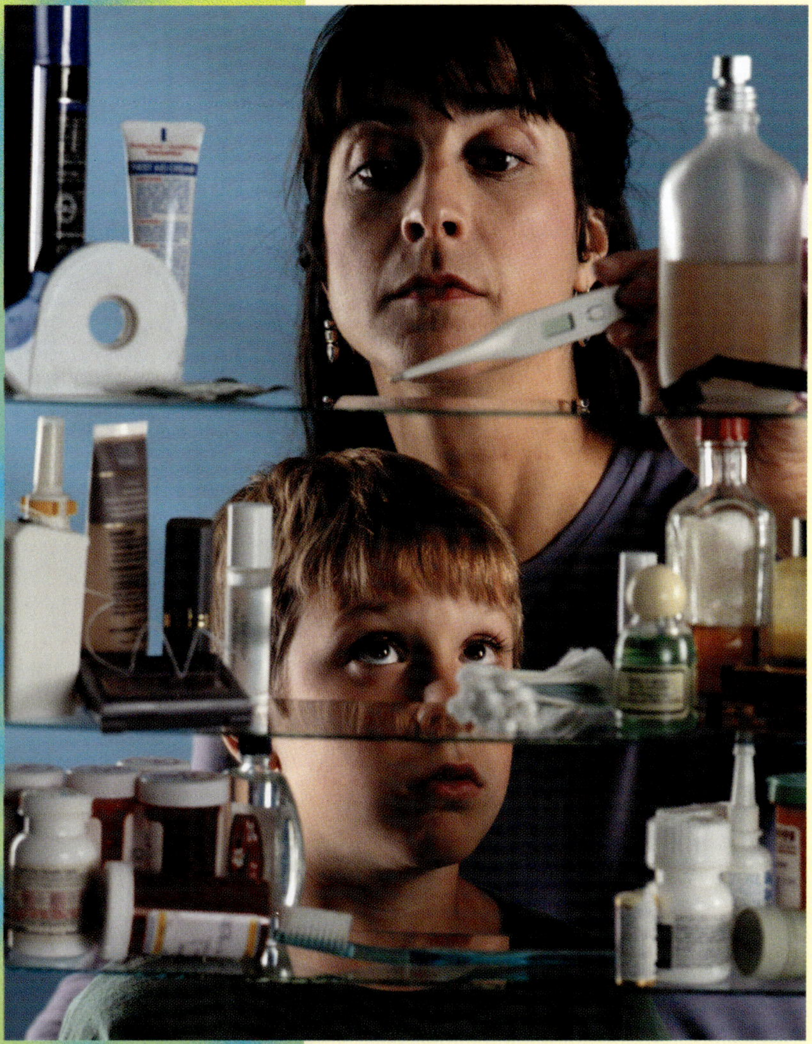

It is for this reason that Tibetan lamas constantly stress the essential foundation path of Buddhism and especially Bodhicitta and Sunyata. To have practised and developed some realisation in these things is vital, before considering tantra:

Bodhicitta; out of great gratitude for the kindness of every sentient being in this and past lifetimes, I will not enter the final state of enlightenment until every one of them is enlightened.

Sunyata; in an ultimate sense all is empty and empty of its own emptiness. Therefore all I visualise comes out of and returns to ever-present emptiness in the lotus of compassion.

The power of rock, film and sports stars to inspire is so great that many have taken on the status of religious icons in the minds of their followers. Fans are attracted and seek to ride on the sensuality of the glamour. The unity of togetherness at a major performance creates a totality that can seem like enlightenment, but will it last once we are not there, or with the people who were there? So we spend our lives trying to recreate what can never be again.

Left and below: images of beauty, fun, fear, humour, loyalty and family responsibility are hijacked to ensure we buy this and that object, holiday, insurance policy and so on.

Contrast this to our world today, where sensual attachment is used to manipulate and speed us towards all kinds of goals, as if every one of them were an absolute and eternal truth that could make us happy forever. Images of beauty, fun, fear, humour, loyalty and family responsibility are hijacked to ensure we buy this and that object, holiday, insurance policy and so on. Clearly we need to drink large quantities of alcohol, or wear certain clothes, or listen to particular music to have attractive friends! Children are made to feel outsiders, if they are not interested in at least one of the in-fashion activities. Because the juices of wanting are activated, the urgency "to have" is accelerated.

Below: to sing-a-long about the unity and togetherness of our group of believers, then listen to statements of hatred and condemnation of other groups is probably the most dangerous and destructive of activities.

In social and political life similar abuses occur. The scaremongering and inflated offers of politicians, lobbyists and activists are well known. Some religious practices can be even more dangerous. To sing-a-long about the unity and togetherness of our group of believers, then listen to statements of hatred and condemnation of other groups is probably the most dangerous and destructive of activities.

It has been the root power that has driven intolerance, persecution and war throughout human history. "We seem so right together, only 'evil' people would wish to spoil this." The closer we come to a truth that unites, the more dangerous it is to believe in it – unless that truth unites entirely, because no one will deny it.

Above: entertainment, political, or religious preference is not wrong in itself. It is the absolute attachment to these things and especially giving to them special magical or absolutely important authority, wherein lies the danger.

Not that any form of personal pleasure, entertainment, political, or religious preference is wrong in itself. It is the absolute attachment to these things and especially giving to them special magical or absolutely important authority, wherein lies the danger. In the world seen by the unenlightened mind change is constant – nothing lasts. Suffering is caused by seeking permanence, where only impermanence is possible. Extreme suffering is caused by seeking to force permanence by magical invocation, where only impermanence is possible. The more we sing our star's favourite song, or repeat his slogan; chant an advertising or political jingle; shout out our team's song; repeatedly watch a film; wear, or use that particular product; even "join hands celebrating the lord, or the Goddess, or the Earth" for any reason other than the sheer joy of just doing it, the more we bring the possibility of suffering on ourselves and others. By all means, we should do what we enjoy, but for its own sake without any expectation at all.

For tantra is imagined out of emptiness, solely for the benefit of others. Any merit we receive from its practice is only of use, if we dedicate it. With this in our minds, we practise and accelerate our path to enlightenment for the benefit of all sentient beings.

HH THE DALAI LAMA OF TIBET

*"You are the source of all happiness and goodness.
All-powerful Chenrezig, Tenzin Gyatso,
Please remain until samsara ends."*

From the long-life prayer to HH The Dalai Lama

At dawn in the remote village of Takster in Amdo in Eastern Tibet on 6th July 1935 a boy was born, who was to have a most remarkable destiny. The previous Dalai Lama of Tibet had died and now was the time to find his reincarnation. Various methods of divination were being employed. A visit to a sacred mirror lake gave searchers a picture of a mother and child in a small house with a distinctive garden and roof tiles, down a twisting mountain road from a golden-roofed monastery. When this exact place was found, the boy recognised the lama disguised as a servant, his mala and other objects from the previous incarnation and spoke in a special dialect, unfamiliar to his region. He was recognised and taken to live in the Potala in Lhasa to be educated and prepared for his life as the fourteenth Dalai Lama of Tibet.

Below: monks playing 'dung-chen' or long trumpets before a festival at Nechung Monastery, Tibet.

When His Holiness was 15 and long before his studies were completed, the new Chinese communist government made their moves to invade, or as they saw it "liberate" Tibet. There followed nine years of "cat and mouse" relations with the Chinese, whose presence became more and more dominant. In 1959, it became impossible for The Dalai Lama to remain in Tibet. Having to choose between a bloodbath and exile, he escaped late one night and, after a long and dangerous journey, reached asylum in India.

The 20th century saw numerous surges towards people's democracy and the consequent fall and exile of many sovereigns and absolute rulers. Nearly always, they lived out their lives in comfortable exile, little in the public eye. At the time, The Dalai Lama seemed an ideal candidate for such a fate. Chinese Maoist Communism was the new political reality promising material fairness and prosperity to all without privilege. Many radical westerners thought it would only be a matter of time before it replaced "decadent capitalism". In contrast, the Tibetan state appeared to be an unbelievable anachronism. It was feudal, led by an inexperienced young man, who for "some strange superstitious reason" had been given absolute temporal and spiritual authority. This curiosity from the past had "quite rightly" been swept away.

Below: in the early 1950s the new Chinese communist government made their moves to invade, or as they saw it "liberate" Tibet.

Over the last 40 years or so, things have worked out in completely the opposite way. For while the Chinese continue to occupy Tibet, it is still against the will of the Tibetan people, who remain loyally devoted to The Dalai Lama. The Chinese have had to resort to force of arms, arbitrary imprisonment and mass colonisation to maintain their position. Maoism and Chairman Mao himself have been largely discredited. In spite of its size as a potential market, China still struggles to justify its human rights record and be accepted fully in the world community. In contrast, the Tibetan Buddhist tradition has been regenerated in several parts of India. The knowledge has been adopted by some of the most sensitive and intelligent people from societies all over the world – the very people, who in 1959 it was thought more likely to adopt Maoism!

This unbelievable turnaround has been as a result of the power and profound wisdom of the Buddha Dharma knowledge that this book seeks to introduce. The focus of the resurgence of Tibetan Buddhism in the modern world has been the very special character of the man at its centre – HH The Dalai Lama of Tibet. With a gathering army of lamas, geshes, monks and ordinary people, who chose exile with him,

His Holiness established centres of art, learning and medicine in Northern and Southern India. During the 1960s curious visitors from the west came to learn the language and make contact with this very special knowledge. It had been saved from destruction at Nalanda in Northern India, by being taken to Tibet in the first millennium AD. Now it was being preserved in India and developed in modern 20th-century societies. Lamas were invited to western countries. Visits by His Holiness were arranged. As the 1970s developed into the 1980s and 1990s, many hundreds of centres were established. The Dalai Lama was filling major venues and seeing world religious and political leaders on an increasingly regular basis. Cordial contacts were made with many Chinese societies in South East Asia.

Always at the centre of these developments is this simple man, who speaks of peace and compassion towards all beings, does not excuse the Chinese behaviour in his country, but refuses to advocate insurrection against them. He is able to build bridges between religions, societies and individuals. His simple, almost playfully natural way of interacting

Far left: China still struggles to justify its human rights record and be accepted fully in the world community.

Below: His Holiness the Dalhi Lama with President Nelson Mandela, Cape Town, 1996.

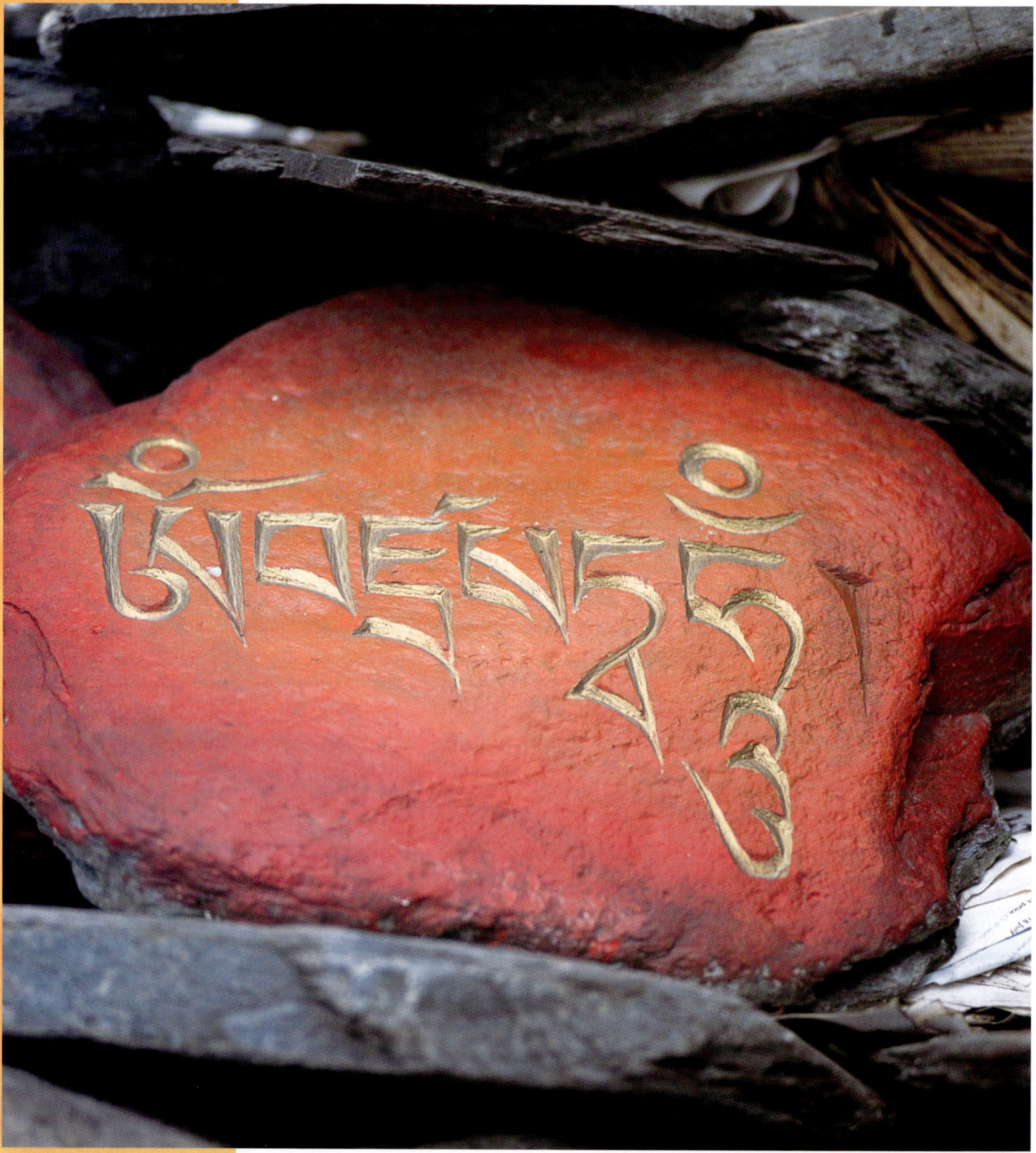
ༀམཎིཔདྨེཧཱུྃ།

with all people moves them toward wonder, relief and compassion for all beings. Everywhere he goes a magical surge of excitement and healing seems to be generated, as people came together. "What is it like being a God-King?" ask the media. He laughs, as if used to being gently overwhelmed, "I see myself as a simple Buddhist monk."

His Holiness The Dalai Lama of Tibet is the recognised living incarnation of Chenrezig, the Buddha of Compassion. Chenrezig has many visual forms. The picture of 1,000 armed Chenrezig explained in Chapter 5 is one of them. The crucial thing is not just the ideal god-like visual appearance, however. It is the effect that practising the ceremony, reciting the mantra, keeping the morality and dedicating all this has. He is the living embodiment of compassion, not because of our blind faith. We are not programmed, or forced to believe anything. He is the living embodiment of compassion, because it is how we feel, when we are near him. The closer we get the more we feel it. This is something he has because of the purity of his practice.

Central to this practice is the mantra OM MANI PADME HUM. OM is the holy body, speech and mind of the Buddha. Some people say it is the sound the earth makes as it moves through space. MANI is the jewel of compassion at one's heart. PADME is the lotus realising the wisdom of emptiness. HUM is the union of compassion and wisdom. Together the mantra invokes, "May the jewel of compassion I hold at my heart open to benefit others". This mantra is repeated trillions of times every year throughout the world and, while it is, HH The Dalai Lama of Tibet will live and benefit us. Like a compassionate mirror he stands gently before us. Kindly he reflects back our behaviour exactly as it is. Meeting him face to face is an experience of simple truth. We find it easy to let go of our delusions and uncertainties. In doing so, we progress toward the clear light of beginningless Buddha mind.

OM MANI
PADME HUM

Far left: 'Om mani padme hum' on a mani stone in Dharamasala, India.

INDEX